A MATTER OF PRINCIPAL

A Former School Principal's Journey
to Redefine Education and Bring
Learning Back to the Home

BY: MANDY DAVIS

To Emma, Clara, and Cruz, the heartbeats of my journey, you've taught me in ways I could never have imagined. And to Josh, my anchor, who saw the vision of our unconventional path even when it wasn't clear to me. This narrative belongs as much to you as it does to me. With all my love, today and forever.

Contents

Part III. Reflections and Revelations

Part IV.
Rediscovering Education's True Essence

Prologue:
A JOURNEY BEYOND TRADITIONAL WALLS

The hum of fluorescent lights, the orchestrated rhythm of bells signaling the start and end of classes, and the palpable energy of hundreds of students navigating their formative years—this was the world that I knew. From my early days teaching up to that first day walking into the building as the new elementary school principal, I was deeply entrenched in the intricate web of our education system.

While I witnessed first hand those classroom and child-specific wins in academia, amidst these triumphs, there were undeniable cracks. Some subtle, others glaringly evident, and over time, these fissures became harder to ignore.

The rigidity of standardized tests, the stifling of individual creativity, and the often one-size-fits-all approach left many students—and educators—feeling disconnected and discontented. The added pressures of the pandemic, with its impact on classroom dynamics and the concerning rise of teacher shortages, only exacerbated these underlying issues. Furthermore, the recent politicking over curriculum choices served as a reminder of the broader debates surrounding the purpose and direction of our education system.

As a seasoned educator, I deeply felt these strains. There were moments of doubt and introspection as I wrestled with each of these systemic challenges. I began to question: was there another path, one that honored the individual child, offering them the freedom and support to thrive not just academically, but holistically?

Seeking answers, I knew that this meant walking away from everything I had ever known. Everything I had dedicated my own education, time, and professional career to build upon.

This internal grappling led me on a profound journey—one that took me beyond the traditional walls of institutionalized education. Leaving behind my role as a principal wasn't a decision made lightly. It was a conscious choice, fueled by my yearning for an educational approach that resonated more deeply with my beliefs.

From the structured corridors of school, I transitioned to the nurturing confines of our home, embarking on a homeschooling adventure that would transform the way I saw *education*. This book is a reflection of that journey and a call for you to reevaluate your own. It's about questioning norms, daring to redefine education, and discovering the profound intersections between formal schooling and homeschooling.

As you delve into these pages, expect a blend of insights, anecdotes, challenges, and revelations. This is not just my story, but a tale of education's evolving landscape, and an invitation to all who believe there's more to learning than what meets the eye.

PART I

UNRAVELING THE THREADS OF TRADITIONAL EDUCATION

CHAPTER ONE

ECHOES FROM THE HALLS: MY LIFE AS A PRINCIPAL

❝

"The function of education is to teach one to think intensively and to think critically. Intelligence plus character—that is the goal of true education."

- Martin Luther King Jr.

he corridors of the school were a microcosm of life. Energetic footfalls of students rushing to classes, whispered secrets exchanged between best friends, the occasional stern voice of a teacher guiding the crowd—these were the melodies of my daily routine.

But there's a texture beneath these sights and sounds that often goes unnoticed. For every child who eagerly answers in class, there's one who hesitates, holding back a reservoir of potential. *How are these children being supported?* For every teacher who enthusiastically follows the curriculum, there's another yearning to break away, to teach what they believe truly matters. *How are these teachers being heard?*

Being the elementary school principal within the walls of your own children's school had its quirks. Picture this: overseeing lunch duty while trying to diplomatically handle your daughter's vehement insistence on trading her apple for a classmate's gummy bears, or sitting through a parent-teacher conference where the teacher is just as nervous about discussing your child's progress as you are. But amidst these humorous and occasionally awkward situations lies an undeniable advantage: the precious opportunity to watch your children grow and learn in real-time, each day.

Everyday presented a new opportunity to pause outside my own children's classrooms, and listen.

While there were some days when the air was filled with the genuine excitement of a child's voice, proudly answering a question or eagerly sharing a personal story, there were also moments dominated by the sound of a teacher's evident frustration or the cacophony that accompanied classroom transitions. The moment I will never forget was the day I heard my own daughter's voice, sounding completely monotonous and detached.

This was not the child I knew.

While both of my girls have always had a love of learning, in this particular instance I knew something was not right. I couldn't help but walk into the room to observe and learn more.

Her very loving teacher continued in a lesson that seemed the norm of any other day—but my daughter's body language continued to unveil more of the story. She had that unmistakable weariness in her eyes, the kind that came from long hours and even longer days. Her once-vibrant expression now seemed dull, and if I was being completely honest, I would say the term "bored" would be a most fitting description.

In hopes of not interrupting the class further, I snuck out, took note of the situation, and addressed my daughter in our next passing.

"When I saw you in class today, you seemed... uninterested. Is everything okay?" Looking down to my eight year old, who had on her overstuffed backpack with even more books in hand, she responded simply.

"Just a normal day."

I was taken aback. This wasn't like Clara. This bright child, who'd often dazzle us with her hunger for knowledge, seemed now a shadow of herself.

"Sweetheart," I began, kneeling to her level, my eyes trying to pierce into her thoughts, "is there anything I can help you with today?"

She hesitated for a moment, then her gaze met mine. "Mom, sometimes it's just...slow. We went over the same thing three times today. I get it the first time, and then I just wait."

A realization dawned upon me: Clara wasn't just uninterested; she was being held back by a pace that didn't cater to her. While this system was designed with the intent of catering to the majority, it inadvertently sidelined those needing extra practice, as well as those like Clara, eager to surge ahead. Clara was yearning to move faster, to dive deeper, but she was tethered by a one-size-fits-all approach. Faced with the palpable frustration etched on my daughter's face, I found myself grappling with a dilemma: how could I address and assuage her feelings in our fleeting moment together?

Noting my pause and concerned expression, before I had the opportunity to try and apply any verbal bandaids to her wounds, she added, "It's fine though, Mom. It's like this every day."

It was in this moment of subtle cues upon reflecting on what I saw and heard that would offer me even more insights to my own child's experience than a report card ever could. Once a position I deemed fortunate, now holding this front row seat to my children's learning felt heart-wrenching, as if this blessing had shifted to burden.

From my vantage point as a principal, I had a bird's eye view of the school's ecosystem. The meetings with enthusiastic teachers presenting new, innovative teaching methods; the concerned parents wanting the best for their children; the myriad policies and rules that, while necessary, often felt constraining. The balance was delicate—ensuring quality education while catering to the diverse needs of students.

Yet, the more entrenched I became in this system, the clearer the challenges became. Not all students thrived in the same environment or at the same pace. Not all teachers felt empowered to adapt their methods. And increasingly, it felt like the "system" was becoming a formidable barrier to true education *and* joy.

Amidst these revelations, a weight pressed on my heart. Doubts, questions, and the echoing concerns of both students and teachers filled my mind. I felt tethered to a system that seemed to resist change, yet the age-old belief echoed around me: "School is essential." But why did I feel so conflicted, and how could something so "essential" leave so many unfulfilled and searching for more?

In our world today, "school" is often elevated to a pedestal. It's seen as the cornerstone of learning, the place where futures are shaped and potentials are unlocked. But as I've journeyed through the realm of education, both as an educator and a parent, I've come to question: why do we equate the structure of school synonymous with true education?

While schools provide a routine—set classes, set times, and, more often than not, set ways of assessing through standardized tests—they only represent a single approach to learning. That's the skeleton, the blueprint. But where's the heart? Education, in its purest form, is far grander. It's the boundless realm of curiosity, the light bulb moments that aren't confined to classroom walls, and the hunger to know more and go deeper. It's the magic in a child's eyes when they finally "get it," the thrill of a teenager diving deep into a newfound interest, and the ever-evolving journey of those who believe learning never stops.

Given this, why do we so often reduce the vastness of education to the limited scope of school, especially when that scope includes narrow metrics like standardized tests? Isn't it time we rethink our priorities?

Recognize that while schools are a vessel, genuine education is the infinite voyage.

Growing up, "education" and "school" seemed like two sides of the same coin. In my mind, they were the same idea that put me on the same mission to enter the world of teaching. But when I took on the role of a school principal, a role filled with responsibility and the daily ebb and flow of school life, those lines started to blur, and then diverge.

Walking through those school halls, I was surrounded by the tangible, often rigid, structures of the schooling system: timetables, curriculums, and all-important standardized tests. But each day, as I interacted with students, I began to feel a growing unease. A disconnect. The classrooms buzzed with activity, yet I couldn't help but wonder: were we truly educating, or were we just going through motions within the confines of what "school" dictated?

As my husband and I sat one evening, chatting about our individual educational journeys, a stark contrast emerged. While I had followed the traditional university route, he had carved a path distinctly his own. He began recounting his early years, and as I listened, I realized his narrative painted a vivid picture of the chasm between structured schooling and true education.

Throughout his childhood, he frequently moved with his family, transitioning from one school to another. With every transition, he often found himself either retracing steps in subjects he'd already covered or feeling lost in the middle of unfamiliar material. The traditional school system, with its structured and state-dependent curriculum, failed to accommodate the inconsistencies in his educational trajectory. These interruptions left noticeable gaps in his schooling.

Yet, intriguingly, these gaps didn't impede his broader education. Instead, they seemed to forge a resilience and self-reliance in him. Rather than relying solely on formal classroom instruction, he cultivated a knack for self-directed learning, seeking out knowledge on his own terms.

Left to his own devices, my husband took the reins of his learning as an adult. He delved into books that intrigued him, embraced hands-on experiences, and sought guidance from those more knowledgeable in areas he was curious about. Absent the confines of a formal educational structure, he honed his ability to adapt, innovate, and think critically. While many would view this nontraditional route with skepticism or even dismissiveness, he steadily carved his own path.

His journey is a living testament to the distinction between institutionalized schooling and genuine, heartfelt education. While schools might guide students down a well-worn path, true education celebrates the unique rhythms of individual growth and discovery. Today, he not only heads a successful business but also possesses an insatiable thirst for knowledge. He embodies the notion that true education extends beyond classroom walls and grading systems—it's about igniting an unyielding passion for learning and wielding it with dedication.

Reflecting upon his journey within my own role in education, I began to more clearly see parallels within the halls of our school each day. The traditional system, heavily reliant on memorization and focused primarily on academic metrics, seemed increasingly restrictive. Its boundaries often threaten to overshadow the core essence of education—the sheer joy of discovering new ideas, the exhilaration when concepts click, and the profound fulfillment derived from genuine understanding. We must always question: are we merely teaching to a system, or are we truly educating the heart and mind?

From the echoing hallways of my former school, a pressing question began to resonate within me: what truly is the purpose of education? Is it solely to mold students into vessels of memorized facts? Or is it meant to delve deeper, touching the unique essence of each individual, nurturing their inherent potential? As my journey evolved, I found myself pondering, can a traditional school system, with its set parameters, genuinely offer the expansive experience that true education promises?

Reflection Questions:

1. Reflect on your school days. Can you identify moments where you felt truly engaged versus moments of detachment? What made the difference?

   ....

   ....

   ....

   ....

2. How do you define the purpose of education? Is it about scores and rankings, or is there a deeper meaning?

   ....

   ....

   ....

   ....

3. Think about a teacher who left a lasting impact on you. What was it about their teaching style or approach that resonated with you?

   ....

   ....

   ....

   ....

CHAPTER TWO

SYSTEMIC SHORTCOMINGS: LIMITATIONS OF TRADITIONAL ENVIRONMENTS

66

"Education is what remains after one has forgotten what one has learned in school."

Albert Einstein

ow beautiful is that familiar scene of sunshine, filtered through classroom windows, casting a warm glow over rows of desks and the eager faces that occupy them. This setting, so often depicted in our minds and media as the epitome of learning, carries with it an ambiance of tradition and nostalgia. Yet, as times change and as our understanding of education evolves, we must confront a critical inquiry beneath this idyllic imagery: is this environment truly conducive to the holistic growth of a child? The traditional educational setting, though long-standing and time-honored, carries with it inherent limitations that warrant deep reflection.

How, as a society, did we get to this place? This place where I felt I had to question everything I have known of education?

It was a chilly autumn morning when I walked through the hallways of the school holding that esteemed title of "Principal." The bell had just rung, signaling the start of the day, and the usual chatter and commotion filled the halls as students hurried to their respective classrooms.

As I passed by Mrs. Anderson's room, a scene caught my eye, prompting me to linger for a moment by the open doorway. There, in the second row, sat little Lily, a bright and curious first-grader who never seemed to run out of wonder. Today, she was eagerly showing her classmates a small model of the solar system her mother had painted on her hand the night before— her tiny fingers tracing the colorful planets with pride.

Her voice was filled with excitement as she recounted the bedtime story her father had told her about little green Martians and moon cheese. Her peers were utterly captivated, their eyes wide with amazement. They began to chime in, sharing their own imaginative tales of stars and galaxies.

But just as the stories began to weave together, forming a beautiful patchwork of childhood wonder, Mrs. Anderson used a verbal cue, signaling the start of the lesson. She gently, yet firmly, reminded Lily that now wasn't the time for space tales. They needed to focus on the day's curriculum, which, with an irony that wasn't lost on me, was an introduction to the planets.

I watched as Lily's enthusiasm waned, her glowing face turning somber. She sat with her hands clasped on her lap and fixed her gaze on the front, where textbook illustrations of the planets were displayed. The transition was jarring—from an animated little storyteller, brimming with her own understanding of space, to just another student, learning facts from a book.

That scene stayed with me throughout the day. It wasn't Mrs. Anderson's fault; she was only following the prescribed curriculum, ensuring that the lesson's objectives were met while working her best to serve all twenty-four students in the classroom. But I couldn't help but wonder, in our bid to maintain order and consistency, were we suppressing the inherent creativity and wonder of our students? Was this structured environment, with its strict schedules and predetermined topics, truly the best space for young minds to soar?

Lily's story was not an isolated incident. Time and again, I had witnessed such moments—instances where the system's rigidity overshadowed a child's natural curiosity. Genuine interests became secondary to the mandatory learning milestones. It made me question the nuances of our current school system, and whether the classroom, as we designed it, truly catered to a child's holistic development.

It was these observations, these seemingly inconspicuous yet profound moments, that seeded my doubts. What a paradox it was, being so embedded within the system, yet starting to question its very essence. But as I was beginning to understand, sometimes, to bring about real transformation, one must first question everything they've believed to be true.

Navigating the traditional education system, I've often bumped into its limitations. Beyond the usual lesson plans and neat classrooms, there's a hidden challenge. While these systems aim high, they sometimes miss out on recognizing each student's unique spark.

The drive to make every student fit and meet a certain standard can squash their natural creativity, their curiosity, and their everyday joy of learning. As our schools place more and more pressure on tests, scores, and the completionist mindset to achieve curriculum on academic timelines, we are witnessing a simultaneous surge in mental health challenges, behavioral issues, and a discontent with the school experience from teachers and students alike.

Learning should revolve around the sheer joy of discovery, punctuated by those exhilarating "aha!" moments. Yet, the looming shadow of grades often dims this enthusiasm. I've encountered students who excel in exams but falter when tasked with practical applications of their knowledge. This disparity underscores a truth: while our system adeptly equips students with textbook knowledge, there's a pressing need to cultivate thinkers, dreamers, and doers who can adeptly maneuver our dynamic world.

Shifting our lens to a pressing dilemma that continues to impact the support of the individual child, one can't help but spotlight the student-to-teacher ratio. A study by the National Education Association has underscored the significant impact of smaller class sizes on student achievement. And yet, ironically, our present conditions are driving educators away at an alarming rate. The exodus of over three hundred thousand teachers between 2020 and 2022 is a glaring testament to this, resulting in burgeoning class sizes that veer further from the ideal.

In classrooms brimming with students, we watch the dilution of individual attention, which in turn places an immense strain on educators, only worsening our teacher shortage. Imagine trying to cater to the diverse needs of a sea of students; it's almost like attempting to hold back a tidal wave with a single hand. All too often, educators are finding themselves pushed to teach to the median, leaving those students outside these central parameters feeling overlooked and underserved.

With schools grappling with teacher shortages and proliferating class sizes, the significance of parents in the educational journey becomes even more pronounced. As a parent, I possess a nuanced understanding of my child's character, aspirations, and specific requirements. However, in the maze of our conventional school framework, this intrinsic knowledge appears to be frequently sidelined or undervalued.

It's quite perplexing to realize that, even with the immense value of parental insights, they're often overshadowed. Sure, there are those annual parent-teacher conferences where my observations might be noted, but how often are they integrated into my child's broader educational plan? This disparity in input and application doesn't merely reduce the potential for tailored learning experiences but overlooks the pivotal role we parents naturally and passionately play in our children's educational odysseys. Every parent hopes for a system where their insights are not just heard but actively applied, recognizing that we too are integral to our children's success in learning.

Before I became "Principal Mom," I was just "Mom." I knew the hallways of my children's school not as an administrator but as a parent. I attended the PTA meetings, sat uncomfortably on the little chairs meant for much smaller humans during parent-teacher conferences, and navigated the carpool lanes like everyone else. But even then, amidst the sea of parents, I felt oddly disconnected, like an outsider looking in.

It's an anomaly when you work in education, but your own children's school experience feels foreign, almost inaccessible. Yes, even as their principal, even when I was in the same building and knew each of the faces in the teachers' lounge, when it came to my own children's education, there was an invisible line that I seemingly could not cross.

I was forced to confront a disconcerting truth: if even my position within the school didn't grant me the access or influence to cater to my own children's individual needs, what hope did other parents hold? The structure seemed to generalize and streamline, prioritizing a "one-size-fits-all" approach. This left little room for recognizing and addressing the unique attributes and requirements of each student.

Throughout the years, I would hear other parents express concerns or share aspirations about their children. Some were heavily involved, spearheading school events or actively participating in classroom activities. Others, busy with their lives, trusted the school to do its job. And yet, there was a general sentiment that, as parents, we had limited sway in the actual curriculum, teaching methods, and daily experiences that shaped our children's lives.

Perhaps what made it even more jarring for me was the stark contrast to my professional environment. In the staff meetings and during curriculum planning, a semblance of control existed. We, as educators, made decisions that impacted students directly. Yet, as a parent, I found myself questioning: where is my voice in this sea of educational influences? Can I make meaningful contributions beyond simply sending in cupcakes for the holiday party?

So there I was, well-versed in the language of education but feeling as if I had no voice in the protection and well-being of my children. And this isn't just my story; it's a shared experience for many parents.

In hindsight, this formative experience as a parent, not as an administrator, added a layer of urgency to my shift towards homeschooling. It wasn't just about the limitations of traditional schooling; it was about reclaiming the narrative of my children's educational journey, and by extension, our family's path.

I had known what a semblance of control looked like from the other side, and I yearned for it, not just for myself, but for every parent who felt their voices were lost in the wind. Because if education is a partnership between schools and families, shouldn't parents be the co-authors of their children's story, rather than just passive spectators?

And finally, when we think about the educational environment, curriculum undoubtedly plays a crucial role in setting the stage. It's not just about the subjects or the lesson plans; it's a reflection of societal values, and sometimes, prevailing political views. Ideally, a curriculum should be about equipping our children with a comprehensive, balanced view of the world, enriching their minds and preparing them for the future. However, external influences can shift this balance.

Such influences can result in certain subjects getting amplified attention, while others might fade into the backdrop. This selective approach to education doesn't just affect knowledge; it shapes the very atmosphere in which our children learn. It's crucial for us to constantly assess and question: by allowing a system to dictate what our children learn, are we genuinely crafting the optimal environment for our kids to flourish and develop?

In this constantly evolving world, where innovation is at the forefront of every field, our educational landscape too begs introspection. I was flooded with an immense passion to take a hard look at our established systems, not only as an educator and school principal, but as a concerned parent with students of school age.

As we reflect on the traditional classroom model, it becomes imperative to ask: is this really the pinnacle of what we can offer our children for their education?

Reflection Questions:

1. How do you feel about the class sizes at your child's school? Do you think your child gets the attention they need?

....

....

....

....

2. How often does your child's school consider your insights or feedback in their teaching approach?

....

....

....

....

3. Have you noticed any external influences or biases in your child's school curriculum? How do they align with your own beliefs or values?

....

....

....

....

CHAPTER THREE

THE ILLUSION OF CONTROL: THE HIERARCHIES OF EDUCATION

66

"Do not confine your children to your own learning, for they were born in another time."

- Hebrew Proverb

tandardization: a term often celebrated in manufacturing and large-scale production. But when applied to the vibrant, dynamic world of education, it can become a double-edged sword. Schools, in their quest for uniformity and consistency, often create molds—predefined shapes into which students are poured, with the expectation that they'll solidify into identical outcomes.

But children are not molten metal, and education isn't a factory line.

In the hustle and bustle of school life, there are those who fit seamlessly into these molds. They thrive in structured environments, ace standardized tests, and march confidently within these set boundaries. But for every one of these students, there is another handful who struggle—**the outliers**.

The outliers are those whose brilliance can't be captured by a letter grade or whose potential is stifled by the constraints of a one-size-fits-all system. Moreover, among these outliers are those who, on the surface, seem to effortlessly fit the mold. Yet beneath this façade, they wage silent battles with their mental well-being.

I was an outlier.

From the early days of my education, I navigated a school environment, not just as a student seeking knowledge, but as a young child seeking acceptance.

Adopted from Seoul, South Korea when I was just three months old, I was one of a handful of non-white students at my elementary school. While it is no secret that children can be cruel, at a very early age, I was introduced to the emotional torment of bullying and the harsh realities of learned resilience.

I would observe other students blending seamlessly into the background, participating without hesitation and enjoying their school days with an ease that eluded me. In stark contrast, my daily reality was punctuated by moments of feeling singled out. The giggles that erupted when I spoke in class, the hushed whispers that followed me in hallways, the stares that lingered just a second too long—every day was a lesson in endurance.

While the classroom offered wonder and insights to those that comfortably fit the mold of the average student, it was this same setting that became my daily battlefield.

There were children who, in their innocence or ignorance, pulled at the corners of their eyes or tried to mimic languages they didn't understand. Their actions, whether playful or mean-spirited, left scars that lingered well beyond school hours.

It baffled me. How could this place where I was supposed to learn about the world and become the best version of myself, instead make me feel so alienated and alone? Questioning my own self worth, I came to ask myself later in life, "Where were all the adults?"

While I could have let this pain and isolation consume me, because I was blessed with a supportive and loving home life, I was able to change this pain to passion. A fervor to ensure that no child ever felt unseen or unaccepted in this very place meant for growth. Driving me towards a career in education, I wanted to make a difference in this broken system.

This was my starting block.

Never did I expect, even as an adult, to continue to feel like an outlier in a system that continued to call for conformity.

As school principal, I saw the outliers, struggling with different yet similar themes than my own. I remember Logan, a bright-eyed third grader with an insatiable curiosity about the world. He'd often wander off during recess, exploring every nook and cranny of the school grounds, only to be reprimanded for not "playing properly." Then there was Talia, a gifted storyteller. She could weave tales that transported her listeners to other worlds, but struggled with the rigid structures of essay writing, leading to mediocre grades and diminishing confidence.

Teachers, too, felt the pressure of these molds. Ms. Smith, with her passion for outdoor learning, often expressed her wish to take her lessons beyond the four walls, to let children learn from nature. But curricular demands and tight schedules made her innovative methods a fleeting dream.

To break away from the preset molds and better serve the outliers, I sought out a firmer understanding of the educational hierarchies stopping us from finding a solution to nurture the inherent individuality of each student and educator.

In the realm of education, hierarchies cascade from a state and federal level, down through districts, school admin, educators, and ultimately to the influence upon the youngest of students. There is a silent narrative suggesting that wisdom also flows top-down—from administrators to teachers, educators to pupils.

However, this belief that those at the top—such as politicians, district leaders, and policymakers—possess superior wisdom can obstruct the very essence of learning. It risks stripping the most vulnerable in the hierarchy—students and their parents—of their rightful control, influence, and capacity for true growth.

Standing amidst these faint cries of help within my own school corridors, I began to question my initial belief. Could I genuinely achieve both outstanding academic results while also nurturing well-rounded individuals? Could the bureaucratic red tape be overcome?

Driven by an insatiable desire to influence and reform, I eagerly dove into the world of education at the young age of twenty-two. Fresh out of college, I was buzzing with the naive optimism of someone who believed they could change the world. Even before the ink on my degree was dry, I secured a position in one of Nebraska's most reputable school

districts. It was an exhilarating time—I was stepping into the professional arena, armed with theories, passion, and a roadmap I believed would lead to success.

Seeing the hierarchy of the educational landscape laid out before me, I interpreted it as a linear progression. Start in the classroom, touching young lives directly. Move up, maybe head a department, contribute to the curriculum. Venture further, into administration, where the broader strokes of educational policies and strategies are crafted. And, if the stars aligned, helm a school as its principal or even influence larger educational policies at the district level. This roadmap, I believed, was the path to making a real difference.

I recall looking up to those in positions of power with a mix of respect and anticipation. They were the decision-makers, the individuals whose vision we implemented. A nod from the principal could make or break an initiative. The decisions from the district office set the course for the academic year. They held, I believed, the tools and authority to effect the most substantial changes. It was towards these echelons of influence that I thought my journey should lead if I wanted my passion for education to truly leave a mark.

Then, I became a parent.

The birth of my children reframed the entire educational ladder. What once was a vertical path now seemed more like a complex web, with each node representing a stakeholder—students, parents, teachers, administrators, and policymakers. The rungs on the ladder were no longer just about *ascending to a higher title, but about depth, influence, and genuine connection.*

As a parent, my concerns weren't about what title someone held but about their impact on my child. A teacher's dedication to understanding my child's unique learning style mattered more than a principal's strategic plan for the school year. The compassion of a school counselor was of greater importance than the latest district-wide initiative. The roles I once viewed as the pinnacle of the educational hierarchy now seemed distant, while those directly interacting with my children became paramount.

Moreover, I began to see the gaps, the disconnects. There were instances when decisions made at the top seemed far removed from the realities of the classroom. Policy choices sometimes felt more influenced by politics or optics than genuine educational needs.

It wasn't a simple switch from viewing one role as more important than another. Instead, it was a profound realization that every role, every position, had its significance, but their impact was felt differently, depending on where you stood. My concern: how would I know which positions, roles, and persons had my children's best interest in mind?

Reflecting upon my journey, from the idealistic educator to a principal, and then to parenthood, a realization dawned. Every hierarchy, in its nature, creates divides. These divides, while initially subtle, can grow and overshadow the primary mission of education. We build systems, structures, and procedures in hopes of streamlining and optimizing. But over time, if not kept in check, these very systems can become limiting, reducing the vibrant, diverse world of education to checkboxes and protocols.

The outliers often illuminate the discrepancies and blind spots within these hierarchies. They challenge the norms, not out of rebellion, but out of a genuine mismatch between their intrinsic nature and the prescribed path. My husband, with his self-taught journey, had been such an outlier. Logan and Talia, with their unique strengths and struggles, were the reminders of the vast spectrum of learners we encounter. Ms. Smith, yearning for the freedom to innovate, represented educators constrained by structures.

All these stories highlight a critical need: to pause, reflect, and reassess. To ask ourselves if we are genuinely nurturing each individual's potential or merely channeling them through a predetermined funnel.

We need a reimagining, a shift from viewing education as a hierarchy to understanding it as a network—a network where connections, interactions, and influences are multi-directional. Where the voice of a third-grader holds as much weight as a district policymaker. Where outliers aren't anomalies but indicators of the diverse tapestry of learners. Where decisions stem from ground realities and are reflective of the diverse needs of the community.

In the end, it isn't about discarding hierarchies, but about refocusing them, ensuring they serve their true purpose: to foster a rich, holistic, and inclusive environment where every individual, regardless of their role, feels valued, understood, and empowered. As we stand at this crossroads, we must ask ourselves: are we shaping our educational systems to truly nurture each individual's potential, or are we merely molding individuals to fit a broken system?

Reflection Questions:

1. Can you recall a time in your educational journey where you felt confined or limited by a "mold?" How did it affect your learning experience?

....

....

....

....

2. How do you think education systems can balance the need for structure with the importance of individuality?

....

....

....

....

3. Who should hold the most responsibility and power of choice when it comes to your child's education?

Do you feel that person/group currently holds this
control?

....

....

....

....

THE MASKS WE WEAR: A PANDEMIC'S AMPLIFICATION OF SYSTEMIC FLAWS

66

"In any given moment we have two options: to step forward into growth or step back into safety."
-Abraham Maslow

he balance between professional dedication and personal devotion is never easy. As a school principal, my role demanded an unwavering commitment to an entire community of students, teachers, and parents. I was deeply entrenched in the school system, perceived as the person whose duty it was to cater to everyone else's needs. But with the birth of my son, a seismic shift occurred in how I viewed that balance.

The joy and challenges that came with my son's arrival brought about a personal awakening. My daughters, already part of the school system, had given me a preview of its strengths and shortcomings. Although I had harbored some concerns regarding facets of their education, my commitment to serving within their school persisted, hoping to be the beacon guiding them through.

Now, holding this sweet newborn in my arms, a new cascade of questions flooded my mind. Was my professional dedication overshadowing my primal role as a mother? Could I be the principal everyone expected while also being the mother my children deserved? While I initially assumed that my position in education would align me more closely with my children's journeys, was I inadvertently creating a greater chasm between us?

Returning to my role of principal with these concerns and questions weighing heavily on my heart, I expected the familiar comfort of my role—the hallways echoing with children's laughter, the sense of purpose that emanated from every classroom, the camaraderie with the staff—would bring me back to peace. What awaited me was far different.

The air was heavy with a palpable tension.

Upon my return, instead of a warm welcome, I faced subtle and not-so-subtle questions about my commitment. My supervisor's inquiries, while seemingly benign, carried an undertone of skepticism. Was my dedication to the school in question just because I took time to nurture my newborn?

In our private Christian school, administrative meetings were a union of both the K-12 educational leadership and the church's hierarchy. Just like in any workplace, I had bonds that ran deep with some, while with others, our interactions barely transcended polite nods during Sunday services.

Yet, despite the varying degrees of camaraderie, we functioned as a unit, and I was deeply committed to our cause. As the clock ticked closer to my first meeting after my maternity leave, a tempest of emotions surged within me. The urgency to pump pressed on both my body and mind; the aching sensation reminding me of the personal sacrifices that came with my position.

Every second that passed was a heartbeat away from my infant son. The looming hour-long meeting meant I would barely get a cherished moment with him before his usual bedtime. The thought of missing nearly all his waking hours was a dagger in my heart, and hoping for just one waking hour with him felt like salt on an open wound.

It's a heartache many working mothers recognize. That yearning to be in two places at once. Wanting to give your all at work, to be the professional everyone expects, while a piece of your heart constantly drifts to the little hands you left at home.

Simultaneously, my phone buzzed with messages from my daughters. They were downstairs in my office, waiting. Their day, like mine, stretched on, keeping them from the fleeting final hours of sunlight and play. Keeping them from time with Daddy and their baby brother at home. They, too, were paying the price of this system, and the buzz of my phone was my reminder of their discontent.

I was drowning in guilt—as a mom, an employee, and a person. My role was meant to offer a balance, a better connection with my family, but instead, I felt the widening gap.

My distracted demeanor didn't go unnoticed. I sensed disapproving glances. And now, the added embarrassment of leaking. This moment underscored the challenging and often conflicting demands of my role, and while I didn't realize it then, that moment was pivotal in my ultimate exit.

My very identity within the institution seemed questioned, and my extended (and unpaid—nod to the USA) maternity leave seemed to diminish my capability as an educator and leader. Each day became a battle to reassert my commitment to the school, all the while the inner turmoil of balancing my roles as a mother and professional grew more intense. With every cold glance or whispered doubt, the disconnect between my personal convictions and the institution's expectations became more evident. To further amplify this tumultuous period, let me highlight that this was in the year of 2021.

On top of my challenging return to the workplace, face masks, once a symbol of medical professions, were now a stark reminder of the changed world we were navigating. And I watched the pandemic continue to transform and control more than just our health protocols—it had shaken the very foundation of the educational system.

The pandemic was not just a health crisis; it was a mirror, reflecting the vulnerabilities in our educational structure. The immediate shutdown of physical school spaces forced a sudden pivot to online learning. This abrupt transition illuminated a stark reality: the digital divide. Not every child had access to devices or stable internet, making remote learning an unattainable luxury for many. It was disheartening to see that our educational ecosystem, which should ideally be an equalizing force, was, in fact, deepening inequalities.

The crisis also exposed the power struggles for control behind the scenes. Decision-making during these trying times revealed the bureaucracy and power plays involved in school governance. The politics of when to open, how to open, and what protocols to follow often overshadowed genuine concerns for student welfare and effective learning; it was an eye-opening realization of just how many strings are attached in the system, and not all are pulled with the best interests of the students in mind.

Moreover, the pandemic revealed the fragility of our "well-oiled" system. It was alarming to witness how a singular unforeseen event could send shockwaves through the entirety of our established educational framework. From canceled examinations to disrupted learning experiences, the tremors were felt at every level.

Watching the world adapt to the whirlwind changes brought on by COVID-19 was a revelation. Families everywhere were thrust into a new way of living, and the lines between work, school, and leisure blurred into one chaotic swirl. Conversations with friends and peers reflected the tumult. There were questions, frustrations, and an overwhelming feeling of being adrift. Many were asking, "Is this what homeschooling feels like?" I found myself pondering the same, knowing the nuances of genuine homeschooling were different.

The confusion was evident. In many households, parents were left scratching their heads: "Am I supposed to be the teacher now? How do I support what the school is sending home? Is this really what homeschooling is about?" Clearly, the pandemic's forced home-learning scenario was not an accurate portrayal of the deliberate and thoughtful approach of authentic homeschooling.

Though our family wasn't homeschooling at that moment, my understanding and empathy for the homeschooling ethos was growing by the day. Observing from the sidelines, I felt the palpable difference between what many were experiencing and the rich tapestry that true homeschooling could weave.

One evening, during a quiet moment of reflection after a heartfelt phone call with a longtime friend, the weight of the situation pressed upon me. My friend, a dedicated professional, shared her day's challenges: juggling work deadlines with her daughter's online assignments, all while trying to keep her toddler entertained. "I'm drained," she admitted, her voice quivering with a mix of fatigue and desperation. "This isn't schooling or working. It's just...surviving."

It hit me hard. If this emergency transition to "home-based school" was so disorienting for many, how much clarity did they have about authentic homeschooling? This realization deepened my resolve to later share the real essence of homeschooling—far removed from the frantic, unplanned scramble many found themselves in. It's not just about bringing school home; it's about crafting a meaningful, flexible learning journey centered around our children. And as challenging as the pandemic was, it also offered a chance to reflect on our choices and the potential paths of education we might choose for the future.

In retrospect, this period of upheaval was a profound learning experience in itself. It underscored the need for a more resilient, inclusive, and adaptable education system, and only magnified my existing concerns about the direction our education system was taking.

While I had long harbored reservations about the broader systemic issues that seemed to place bureaucracy over true education, these new happenings left me feeling unwanted, unappreciated, and completely out of control within my role. These were not just abstract concerns; they were grounded in daily observations, interactions, and the very ethos that surrounded us.

Thus amidst the personal revelations of motherhood and the wider chaos unleashed by the pandemic, I found myself on a precipice. The two worlds—one of intimate personal transformation and the other of global upheaval—intersected, amplifying the pressures of my professional return. The compounded challenges highlighted deep-rooted disparities in expectations and support. At this crossroads, I was compelled to confront and reevaluate my path. This junction, so steeped in emotion and circumstance, became the undeniable catalyst for my momentous decision.

On a particularly heavy evening after work, as the house settled in the silence of exhaustion, my husband and I sat down. Not even needing to exchange many words, the weight of the decision of me leaving my role lingered in the air between us. The stark contrast between the school system's demands and our family's genuine needs was glaringly apparent. We both recognized that the path we were on was unsustainable for the wholesome family life we envisioned.

I was physically worn out, with every muscle echoing the fatigue, and emotionally shattered, feeling like a glass that had been chipped away at until it finally cracked. The daily grind wasn't just a phrase—it was an oppressive, tangible weight, pressing down on my shoulders and refusing to relent. The systemic pressures and ever-looming responsibilities had left me gasping for breath, like a fish out of water, desperately trying to find my grounding.

This strain didn't stay confined to the walls of the school; it seeped into the sanctity of my home. It manifested in ways that eerily mirrored the after-school restraint collapse so many parents witness in their children. Just as children often hold in their stresses, only to release them in the safety of their homes, I too found myself coming undone in the very place that should have been my refuge. The raw vulnerability of those moments, the sense of being so out of sync with myself, was like experiencing a storm inside while the world outside remained oblivious. It was a maelstrom of emotions, leaving both physical and emotional scars in its wake.

The next realization hit hard: if an environment was taking such a toll on me, how could I, in good conscience, let my children be a part of that same setting?

This profound epiphany became the catalyst for change, and it was time to make a heart-wrenching choice. On one hand was the community I had served and loved—a community that was now viewing me with veiled suspicion. On the other hand was the well-being and future of my children.

The choice became clear. While the transition was painful and meant losing ties with many I held dear, it was a necessary step towards a healthier, more holistic environment for both me and my children. It was a decision rooted not in rebellion, but in love and a profound sense of responsibility.

Reflection Questions:

1. Have you ever been in a situation where your commitment or abilities were questioned based on external circumstances? How did you navigate it?

   ....

   ....

   ....

   ....

2. Reflect on a time when you faced systemic challenges that conflicted with your personal beliefs. How did that shape your decisions and actions?

   ....

   ....

   ....

   ....

3. How has the COVID-19 pandemic shifted your perspective on traditional systems, be it in education or other areas of life?

   ....

   ....

   ....

   ....

PART II

THE LEAP INTO THE UNKNOWN

CHAPTER FIVE

FIRST STEPS: NAVIGATING THE NEW NORMAL OF HOMESCHOOLING

66

"The only way to make sense out of change is to plunge into it, move with it, and join the dance."

- Alan Watts

It was an unusual feeling—the culmination of my hard work and years in education, packed into cardboard boxes and the stillness of my once-bustling office. The walls that had witnessed countless meetings, discussions, and decisions, now stood silent. The chair that had been my constant companion through long hours, pregnancy, and my postpartum struggles was vacant.

I hadn't envisioned this day, or at least not as it transpired. In my heart, I never even imagined the time would come to leave—perhaps only one of retirement, with a grand farewell, and an immense sense of both closure and peace. But that's the thing about life: it seldom follows our scripts.

As an introvert, the world often felt loud, and the school system was no exception. Every decision, every meeting, every interaction required a piece of me, leaving me often feeling spread too thin. The constant tug-of-war between my professional responsibilities and my inner self had always been a challenge. But now, the weight of the system felt too heavy, the disparity between what I knew to be right for students and what was demanded of me too vast.

The final decision to leave didn't come after some dramatic event or long deliberation. It was rather an accumulation of small moments, feelings, and incidents that nudged me toward this path. And when the realization hit, it was sudden and clear, like the breaking of dawn after a long, dark night.

I remember the exact moment I knew. Standing in the warmth of the early June sun, I would leave for the summer, and I wouldn't be back. The decision to prioritize my family and personal well-being had been made. There wasn't a grand announcement, no extended farewells, no tearful goodbyes. Perhaps, deep down, I didn't know how to voice the whirlwind of emotions I felt. But I also didn't know I was leaving until I knew.

Walking out of that building, the door clicking shut behind me, I felt a rush of emotions. There was sadness, yes, but also a feeling I hadn't truly felt in years: empowerment. It was the kind of empowerment that comes from making a choice that aligns with one's deepest truths, even if it's a tough one. I hadn't just left a job; I had chosen a path that felt right for my family and me.

Did I handle it perfectly? Probably not. But in that moment, perfection wasn't the goal. Authenticity was. For the first time in a long while, I felt I was steering the ship of my life, rather than being tossed by the waves of external expectations. The future was uncertain, but it was mine to shape.

Driving away from the school, I called my husband.

"Done," was all I said when he picked up.

He paused for just a moment, processing the weight of that single word, then replied, "Onward."

In that concise exchange, the depth of our understanding was evident.

No lengthy conversation was needed. We were united in our path forward, ready for whatever lay ahead.

hange, while inevitable, is seldom easy. Leaving behind the title of "Principal," a role I had passionately worked towards for years, felt like shedding a part of my identity. The school's walls, which once echoed my decisions and ideas, became a distant memory. Yet, with every ending comes a new beginning.

The homeschooling journey, at its outset, felt like navigating uncharted territory. The vast expanse of curriculum choices, teaching methodologies that took a wide range of approaches that seemed foreign to even a former educator, and daily schedules stretched out before me. The comforting routine of school bells, timetables, and parent-teacher meetings were replaced by the fluidity of child-led exploration, spontaneous learning moments, and the ever-evolving dynamics of mother-child interaction.

As I navigated our first year of homeschooling, my years in education began to serve as both a compass and a cautionary tale. Having stood at the crossroads of structured learning, I remembered the moments of triumph when children's passions were stoked and also the disheartening times when their enthusiasm waned under the immense pressure of relentless testing.

This intimate understanding of the traditional schooling system's strengths and flaws provided me with a unique perspective. Instead of being trapped by its limitations, I could harness the best lessons and mold them into our homeschooling framework. It wasn't about reinventing the wheel, but rather, taking my past experiences in education and adapting them to create a tailored, enriching experience at home. And through this process, a series of enlightening lessons began to emerge.

No two children are identical. This much is clear. Within a typical classroom, the relentless march towards uniform benchmarks often overlooks the individual learning curves of each child. In contrast, our homeschool environment sought to cherish and nurture the distinct learning paths my daughters embarked on. While some curricula chase a one-size-fits-all model, we've seen firsthand how honoring individual strengths and curiosities can unlock boundless potential.

Creativity can't thrive within too-tight constraints. In a system that prioritizes set patterns and structures, the spontaneous spark of creativity often gets snuffed out. Yet, within the embrace of our home, we welcome imaginative leaps and bounds. We recognize that creativity isn't a diversion from learning but rather a path to deeper understanding. These unstructured moments, free from the binds of stringent lesson plans, have birthed some of our most profound learning experiences.

Metrics were taking center stage, often sidelining the authentic joy of learning. Yet, in our homeschool haven, we choose to elevate the journey over the destination. Instead of rigid metrics dictating our progress, our compass is curiosity, comprehension, and genuine understanding. Such a holistic approach not only enriches our learning experiences but also cultivates a deeper love and appreciation for the world of knowledge.

Life doesn't fit neatly into boxes. While traditional educational models might push for standardization, our homeschooling journey prioritizes real-world experiences and life skills. We believe that true education is about more than just academic milestones. By emphasizing skills like empathy, resilience, and critical thinking, we prepare our children for life's myriad of challenges, ensuring they become not just knowledgeable, but also wise and compassionate individuals.

Structured learning certainly has its merits, but its defined boundaries often cast shadows over the vast, vibrant world of education. Each day, as I navigate this fresh path, I'm reminded that true learning is a journey, not merely a destination. It's a voyage I want my children to savor.

Guided by this understanding, I shifted my aim. Instead of mimicking the traditional school setting at home, I designed an environment brimming with flexibility, warmth, and sensitivity to my children's unique needs and questions. We plunged into topics that sparked their enthusiasm, paused when they needed to breathe, and consistently celebrated the joy of the journey over the destination.

The freedom homeschooling unveiled was nothing short of transformative. Untethered by the rigidity of conventional systems, the world became our classroom. Nature walks transitioned into immersive biology lessons, kitchen escapades morphed into hands-on chemistry labs, and evening tales ignited in-depth conversations on history, ethics, and life's mysteries.

Our challenges? There have been many, and they continue to evolve. The complexities of balancing numerous roles within the home, occasional feelings of isolation, and the weight of being the primary architect of my children's educational journey are realities I grapple with daily. Yet, it is this unfamiliar territory, transitioning from a structured educational environment to a realm where I have little precedent, that presents the most distinct challenges.

Navigating the Transition: A Former Educator's Unique Challenges in First-Year Homeschooling

1. **Redefining Structure:** With years spent adhering to and managing a strict school schedule, transitioning to the flexible world of homeschooling was an adjustment. Finding the balance between routine and spontaneity, without the confines of bell schedules, took time.

2. **From Classroom Management to Individualized Attention:** Managing a classroom of diverse learners is a stark contrast to focusing deeply on one's own children. There were moments I had to stop myself from taking a broad approach and instead delve deep into personalizing lessons for each child.

3. **Reassessing Pedagogies:** The methodologies and strategies that worked in a classroom setting weren't always effective in the intimate homeschool environment. I found myself constantly revisiting and reworking my approach.

4. **Addressing Expectations:** As a seasoned educator, there was an inherent pressure (often self-imposed) to ensure my children received an education on par, if not better, than what they'd receive in a traditional setting.

5. **Avoiding the Over-Planning Pitfall:** My instinct, honed from years in the education system, was to over-plan. The beauty of homeschooling lay in its spontaneity and organic learning moments, which meant I had to consciously step back at times.

6. **Balancing the Dual Role:** The line between "mom" and "teacher" sometimes blurred. While it was a privilege to be both, it demanded a mental switch— understanding when to don the hat of the nurturing mother and when to step into the shoes of the focused educator.

7. **Handling External Skepticism:** Given my professional background, there were inevitable questions and skepticism from peers in the educational community about my choice to homeschool. Addressing these, while staying true to my decision, was a journey in itself.

8. **Overcoming Resource Overload:** With my deep knowledge of educational resources, there was a temptation to incorporate everything. Sifting through and selecting what truly benefited our homeschooling journey became crucial.

9. **Letting Go of the "Ideal" Curriculum:** With experience in curriculum design and understanding of state standards, it was a challenge to let go of the "perfect" curriculum and instead craft one that was

fluid, dynamic, and tailored to my children's evolving needs.

10. **Embracing a Holistic Approach:** While academics were second nature to me, integrating life skills, emotional growth, and experiential learning into our day-to-day required a broader perspective shift.

The transition to homeschooling was not without its unique challenges. However, every obstacle encountered became a stepping stone, refining our homeschooling approach and deepening the bond with my children. As days melded into weeks and weeks flowed into months, a distinctive rhythm to our homeschooling began to emerge. Initial doubts and uncertainties slowly transformed, replaced by a blossoming confidence and a heart overflowing with joy.

Reflection Questions:

1. Think of a time you embarked on a new journey or venture. What were the initial challenges you faced, and how did you overcome them?

....

....

....

....

2. How do you balance the roles and responsibilities in your home when they seem to overlap or conflict with each other?

....

....

....

....

3. Reflect on the freedoms and constraints in your current learning or professional environment. How do they shape your experience?

....

....

....

....

CHAPTER SIX

BEYOND TEXTBOOKS: THE WORLD AS OUR CLASSROOM

66

"Call it a clan, call it a network, call it a tribe, call it a family. Whatever you call it, whoever you are, you need one."

- Jane Howard

here's a peculiar sensation that accompanies profound change: the simultaneous loss and gain, like two sides of a coin. On one side, there's the palpable excitement of new beginnings, fresh experiences, and uncharted territory. On the flip side, there's the often silent, subtle pain of what was left behind.

The decision to homeschool, while liberating, also evoked a deep sense of isolation in the initial days. The bustling school corridors, friendly banter with colleagues, and the reassuring presence of a larger community were aspects of my previous role that I missed the most. It made me ponder: how do we foster a sense of belonging when the traditional structures of community are absent?

The answer lay in the very essence of homeschooling—forging one's path.

Stepping away from a long-established career felt like removing a part of my identity. Like ripping off a bandaid to a wound I didn't even know existed, the weight of that decision pressed down on me with a mixture of uncertainty, fear, and nostalgia. It wasn't just a job I was leaving behind; it was friends who had become family, co-workers who had shared the highs and lows of my professional journey, and an entire church community that had been our anchor for so long.

And something not often enough talked about is how heavy this isolation, and more so, shielding this isolation of transition, change, and judgment can be on our shoulders, when protecting it from our children. As they watched gatherings with family friends dwindle and invitations to family gatherings cease, my husband Josh and I worked to keep positive and keep this burden from their young minds.

It wasn't just about adapting to a new way of learning; it was about navigating the complexities of human relationships, of understanding the nuances of loyalties and choices. The silence of lost friendships echoed louder than any words spoken. Our children, with their innate sense of empathy and observation, had their own questions:"Why haven't we seen them in a while? Do they not like us anymore?"

In between these inquiries from our children lay a broader societal question: the still-prevailing misconceptions around homeschooling. Even as homeschooling gains traction, it remains an enigma for many, and all the more so in a community where I was known first and foremost as the school principal.

To most, I was defying the very essence of what I had once stood for. The contrast in our choice made others uncomfortable, and it created an undercurrent of judgment and uncertainty. But how do you explain this to children?

The weight of these absences, of explaining without laying blame or introducing bitterness, was one of the hardest tasks I've ever faced. Each time, we chose to emphasize the love and bond within our family, and the understanding that sometimes, people make choices that take them on different paths.

We filled our days building our connections within and filling time with new adventures and new pursuits. Activities that once revolved around community events were replaced with intimate family outings, deep conversations, and explorations of our own strengths and passions. It was through these efforts that we had the opportunity to lean into one of the greatest freedoms of homeschooling, and eventually, we moved forward, finding our new community.

Despite my introverted nature, I embarked on a mission to actively cultivate connections within the homeschooling community. With three children spanning over a decade in age differences, I had concerns that traditional co-op and in-person meet-up options might not be an ideal fit in our first year of homeschooling. Grappling with the ever-present fear of whether I was making the right decision for my children's education, I turned to the boundless world of the internet.

Social media platforms, online forums, and homeschool mom groups became my initial gateway to a thriving community. It was a safe haven where I could candidly share my experiences, ask questions, and gain knowledge from seasoned homeschoolers.

The hum of my phone signaled yet another notification. I had grown accustomed to these constant buzzes, often dismissing them as another bout of digital noise. But as I navigated the unfamiliar waters of homeschooling, my phone, particularly one app, took on a transformative role: Instagram.

In a world often critical of social media's grip on our lives, casting it as a realm of vanity and endless scrolling, I found an unexpected sanctuary. There I was, fresh on a journey less traveled by those in my immediate circles, feeling the weight of isolation. Who would understand the challenges, the joys, the intricate dance of being both a parent and an educator to your own child?

As I began to post snippets of our homeschooling journey, from the meticulously planned lessons to the impromptu science experiments on the kitchen counter, something magical happened. The vast digital expanse of Instagram began to mirror images of families, just like mine, embarking on similar quests. Their living rooms transformed into classrooms, their backyards into elaborate playgrounds of discovery. Every post was a window into another world, yet so strikingly familiar.

It wasn't just about the double taps, the likes, or the follower count. Each comment on a post became a conversation, a tip, an affirmation. From across the globe, I connected with parents who, just like me, were navigating this intricate dance. We celebrated each other's successes, offered solace during challenging times, and shared resources that made our roles just a bit easier.

The beauty of this digital community was its raw authenticity. Gone were the picture-perfect images of textbook homeschooling. In its place were candid shots of real life—messy, unpredictable, yet filled with moments of profound beauty. As I poured out my passion, my uncertainties, and my moments of triumph, I received in return an outpouring of support, wisdom, and camaraderie.

This experience reshaped my perspective on social media. I discovered its potential to be a powerful tool for connection. When approached with intention and genuine authenticity, platforms like Instagram can build bridges, transcending geographical boundaries and forging bonds of shared experience. I learned that when you channel positive energy and genuine intent into the virtual world, it echoes back with a resonance that can deeply enrich your real-world journey.

In this vast sea of hashtags and filters, I found more than just "followers." I discovered a tribe, a community. A group of like-minded souls who reminded me that while our paths might be unconventional, we never walk them alone. And so, amidst the often maligned world of social media, I found a space of empowerment, learning, and profound connection.

Drawing upon the same fervor I once channeled into fostering camaraderie among teachers, I decided to take a bolder step. I transitioned from online interactions to face-to-face collaborations with other homeschooling parents. Stepping out of my introverted comfort zone was not without its challenges, but as time unfolded, I came to appreciate the immense value it brought to both my children and me.

Navigating the world of homeschooling can often feel like a solitary endeavor, a path trodden by courageous parents and dedicated educators, each offering a unique perspective. As I engaged with these diverse families, I discovered that each one contributed a distinct chapter to the ever-evolving story of homeschooling. The collective experiences, methodologies, and journeys of each family added invaluable pages to my own repository of knowledge.

In our collaborative network, we freely exchanged resources, shared tales of triumph, and even found solace in commiserating over shared challenges. These interactions birthed deep and meaningful friendships, solidifying a strong sense of community. It was within this bond of shared commitment to homeschooling that I discovered a richness that went beyond my expectations. This camaraderie not only fortified my dedication to homeschooling but also continued to enhance the overall experience. Diverse perspectives intertwined seamlessly into a cohesive approach to education that celebrated each child's uniqueness.

As our collaborative community thrived, the boundaries of our classroom expanded far beyond the confines of our homes. Joint field trips, group projects, and co-op classes became not only tools for learning but also avenues for my children to interact, flourish, and gain knowledge alongside others who shared this same educational journey. Our community championed a child-centric, customized approach to education, enriched by the collective wisdom of like-minded parents and educators.

Connection Points for New Homeschooling Parents

1. **Social Media Groups:** Join homeschooling Facebook groups, Instagram accounts, or Twitter threads dedicated to homeschooling. These platforms often have vibrant communities of homeschooling parents sharing resources, advice, and experiences.

2. **Online Forums:** Participate in online homeschooling forums to connect with other parents in your area and nationwide. These forums provide a space to ask questions, seek guidance, and connect with other homeschoolers.

3. **Local Homeschool Associations:** Research and connect with local homeschool associations or co-ops in your area. These organizations often host events, field trips, and activities for homeschooling families.

4. **Wild + Free Community:** Explore the Wild + Free Community, an inclusive and nature-inspired homeschooling movement. They offer local groups, online conferences, and resources to support a nature-based, homeschooling lifestyle.

5. **Online/In-Person Homeschool Conferences:** Attend online homeschool conferences and summits. These events bring together homeschooling parents, speakers, and experts, allowing you to learn, connect, and gain inspiration.

6. **Cooperative Learning Groups:** Consider joining or starting a homeschool co-op with other families in your area. Co-ops provide opportunities for group learning, socialization, and shared teaching responsibilities.

7. **Online Classes:** Enroll your child in online classes or courses. This can be a way for them to connect with other homeschoolers while learning specific subjects or skills.

8. **Homeschooling Associations:** Join national or regional homeschooling associations, like the Home School Legal Defense Association (HSLDA) or state-specific organizations. They often offer resources and connections.

9. **Local Sports and Arts Programs:** Enroll your children in local sports teams, art classes, or music lessons. This can be an excellent way for kids to socialize while pursuing their interests.

10. **Book Clubs:** Look for homeschooling book clubs or reading groups in your area or online. Reading and discussing books with other homeschoolers can foster connections.

In essence, while the choice to homeschool might stem from individual family preferences and needs, the journey itself thrives on community. Collaborating with other homeschooling parents transforms this path from a solo endeavor into a shared voyage, brimming with collective wisdom, mutual support, and a shared commitment to holistic learning.

As days turned to weeks and weeks to months, it occurred to me: communities aren't static. They evolve, shift, and transform. While my school was a significant part of my life, it was not my entire life. In stepping away, I had not lost a community; I had merely transitioned to a new one, enriched by diverse experiences and bound by shared convictions.

The world was our classroom, and our community was as diverse as it could get. From seasoned homeschooling veterans to families just starting, from artists and scientists to entrepreneurs and writers, our tribe was a vibrant tapestry of backgrounds and beliefs. While the pain of leaving something you love never truly dissipates, it gets juxtaposed with the joy of new discoveries, fresh connections, and the promise of growth.

Reflection Questions:

1. Reflect on the communities you are a part of. What do they bring to your life?

....

....

....

....

2. How do you nurture and maintain connections in a world that's increasingly virtual?

....

....

....

....

3. Think about a time you felt isolated or out of place. How did you overcome that feeling and find your tribe?

....

....

....

....

CHAPTER SEVEN

FOLLOWING THEIR LEAD: THE NATURAL PATH OF CURIOSITY

66

"Success is not final, failure is not fatal: It is the courage to continue that counts."

- Winston S. Churchill

n the traditional school system, success is often delineated by report cards, test scores, and class rankings. These metrics, while providing a certain measure of a student's academic prowess, rarely capture the holistic essence of growth, curiosity, and individuality.

Transitioning from a structured environment—where such metrics were pivotal—to homeschooling required a paradigm shift in, not only how I perceived success, but how I translated this success onto my children. It was no longer about reaching a specific grade or score but about nurturing a love for learning, fostering resilience, and cultivating critical thinking skills.

Diving into the realm of education back in 2008, I stood at the classroom's threshold, fueled with youthful energy and determination. Fresh from college, brimming with the latest teaching philosophies and a head full of ideals, I was at the forefront, steering a diverse group of keen young learners. My passion was irrefutable, but so was my inexperience.

It wasn't long before I was introduced to the ritual of parent-teacher conferences. I remember the first one vividly. The classroom, usually filled with chatter and energy, felt starkly different that evening. Instead, filled with rows of chairs occupied by parents, each waiting their turn, the room was flooded with palpable tension.

As they approached my desk, clutching the report cards I'd prepared, I could see the concern in their eyes. Their children's futures seemed to hinge on the letters and numbers I had assigned. Mrs. Johnson asked why her son, who had narrated the most incredible stories at home, only received a "B" in writing. Mr. and Mrs. Patel wanted to understand the "C" in math when their daughter had scored well in previous state math exams.

Facing them, I felt the weight of their expectations and the responsibility of my role. Here I was, a young adult without children of my own, trying to explain and justify the worth of their precious children through mere grades and test scores. Adding to this weight was the knowledge that in the upcoming months, I had the added pressure to teach my class the specific content they needed to pass state testing. Even if it meant pushing through material that might not be retained, it was a necessity to ensure students passed, parents remained content, and our school maintained its funding.

That evening was a turning point for me. I came to grips with the inadequacies of a traditional grading system I had once embraced without skepticism. It failed to truly understand the essence, the spirit, and the boundless potential of these young souls. Over the next year of teaching, I felt an even deeper commitment to my students and the inherent flaws of the educational system they navigated.

This profound realization and responsibility drove me to further my education, leading to my pursuit of a master's degree and eventually, an Ed.D/ Ph.D. My ambition at the time was clear: to rise within the system, believing that the right position in administration could offer the leverage needed to introduce meaningful change. However, the further I climbed, the more I began to understand the complexity and rigidity of the system. The belief I held, that change could be brought from within, began to waver. No matter the position or power, some structures, I came to see, were just too entrenched to be truly transformed.

When we first embarked on our homeschooling journey, I knew the majority of my time would be in leaning into changing thought processes and approaches to education that had been ingrained within me for years through my own education and pedagogy. I took time to observe, not just my children's learning styles, but those special sparks of interest, aiming to discern passing fascinations from deeper passions. In order to be their best guide, I needed to understand their approach to learning and interests first.

It was on one of those usual slow mornings that my daughter's eyes shone with unparalleled excitement at the mention of 3D printing. Rather than letting this curiosity fade, I chose to nurture it. We started exploring, initially with library visits that turned into deep dives into books on 3D printing, followed by many evenings spent researching prototyping and the potential of this technology.

For her, this wasn't just another topic. It was an exploration led by her genuine interest, an opportunity for her to take the reins and lead her own learning. The gauge of her success wasn't a standardized test at the end of a unit, but rather the depth of her questions, the meticulousness of her prototype designs, and the evident passion with which she pursued every new piece of information.

Likewise, my older daughter's inclination towards literature became undeniable. The world of words beckoned her, and together, we plunged into classics, exploring themes, dissecting character arcs, and understanding narratives. Her response? She began crafting her own tales, reflecting both her readings and her blossoming imagination.

These experiences underscored an educational philosophy I'd long studied but only now truly embraced: the power of child-led learning. This approach, at its heart, is about harnessing and amplifying a child's natural inquisitiveness. Within the confines of a traditional classroom, there are undeniable constraints revolving around time, support, and access. While standardized lessons often suppress these bursts of curiosity, we had a new freedom to explore.

Pillars of Child-Led Learning

1. **Trust in the Child:** Believe that every child has an innate curiosity and drive to learn. Trust them to know what interests them and what they're ready to learn next.

2. **Respect for Autonomy:** Recognize that children should have a say in their own educational journey. Their voices, choices, and opinions matter.

3. **Learning through Play:** Understand that play isn't just leisure; it's a vital method of exploration and learning for children. It's through play that children often grasp complex concepts.

4. **Flexibility:** Instead of a rigid curriculum, be ready to adapt and change based on the child's evolving interests and needs.

5. **Facilitation, Not Direction:** Parents and educators serve as guides, providing resources, answering questions, and offering support, rather than dictating what should be learned.

6. **Environment Matters:** Create a stimulating environment filled with diverse resources to help nurture a child's curiosity.

7. **Value the Process:** Instead of focusing solely on end results or products, appreciate the learning journey itself—the exploration, mistakes, and discoveries.

8. **Reflect and Review:** Periodically review and reflect with the child on their learning experiences, ensuring they're feeling satisfied and recognizing their own progress.

9. **Holistic Growth:** Beyond academics, emphasize the development of emotional, social, and physical skills.

10. **Community Engagement:** Engage with the world, letting children learn from their community, nature, and real-world experiences.

11. Encouraging Questions: Foster an environment where questions are encouraged. A curious mind is an active mind.

12. Patience and Understanding: Remember that every child's journey is unique. Celebrate milestones, no matter how small, and understand that there might be times of intense interest in a topic and other times of rest.

As we continued to adjust the flow of our homeschool to meet the needs of both the individual and the family, the value of this child-led approach became indisputable. Here, learning was akin to nurturing a flame, not just filling a predetermined mold. In this environment, my children were not just passive learners but enthusiastic explorers charting their unique academic terrains.

My role as both educator and parent in the home pivots from being a director to a facilitator. We're not there to dictate but to guide, provide resources, pose challenging questions, and at times, simply step back, letting them grapple with their questions and find their answers.

In the heart of my fifth-grade classroom, the clock seemed to tick faster than anywhere else in the world. Rows of desks, each occupied by an eager mind, stretched before me. But as the weeks unfolded and the pressure of standardized curriculum and testing loomed, the spirit of this room transformed. The beauty of spontaneous queries and the potential of organic,

child-led learning began to be overshadowed by the relentless march of the academic calendar.

Every day, a carefully planned lesson awaited the students and me. Each topic, each discussion, each activity was designed to fit into a tight schedule—a schedule that was set not by the rhythm of my students' curiosities, but by the demands of a larger educational system. There was always another chapter to finish, another concept to cover, and, before we knew it, another test to prepare for.

I remember one day, in the middle of a lesson on the Civil War, a young boy named Liam raised his hand. "I have a question," he said, his voice filled with genuine curiosity. "Why did people believe so strongly in their side that they were willing to go to war with their own countrymen?" It was a deep question, one that hinted at a desire to understand the emotional and human side of history, not just the dates and facts.

But glancing at the clock and thinking of the pages we still had to cover that day, I had to give him a condensed version of the answer. "That's a complex issue, Liam," I said. "Different people had different beliefs and motivations. We can chat more after class if you'd like." But deep down, I knew we'd both be swept up in the wave of the next class, the next lesson, the next task. That moment of potential deep connection and learning was lost.

This pattern repeated itself more times than I could count. Students, naturally curious, would pose questions or show interest in a tangent that wasn't part of that day's lesson plan. And I, bound by the structure and demands of the system, would often have to redirect them, promising deeper dives that we seldom had time for.

The weight of this reality was heavy. My heart ached to know my students more—not just as learners but as individuals. I wanted to understand their dreams, their fears, and the unique perspectives they brought to our shared space. But the constraints of the classroom, with its fixed schedules and constant push towards standardized testing, made this nearly impossible.

In these moments, the shortcomings of the system became painfully clear. Here were these young minds, eager to understand the world, to ask questions, to dive deep. And there I was, equally eager to guide them, but trapped in a system that often prioritized schedules over genuine, child-led learning. It was a daily struggle, a daily compromise, and a daily reminder of the vast potential that lay just out of reach.

Now, some might raise concerns about ensuring foundational knowledge without a structured curriculum, outside of the confines of a classroom. While foundational knowledge is undeniably essential, it's crucial to understand that true foundational strength isn't just about facts and figures. It's equally about cultivating a genuine love for learning, an attribute that child-led education can nurture like no other.

Our rapidly evolving world further validates this approach. In an age where many future jobs are yet undefined, the true skill will lie in the ability to adapt, learn, and evolve. It reminds me so much of my husband's journey. Just as he charted his own path, often outside traditional frameworks, thriving on self-taught knowledge and adaptability, so too must we prepare our children. Here, child-led learning, emphasizing curiosity and adaptability, holds the key.

Reflecting on my years in the educational arena, memories of that twenty-two-year-old teacher confronted with parents seeking validation through grades and tests come rushing back. The difference is striking. Gone were the days of rote memorization and standardized assessments. Now, I was nurturing thinkers, questioners, and lifelong learners.

As we navigated this path together, it wasn't always smooth sailing. There were days of doubt, days when the old metrics of success tried to cloud my judgment. But with time, patience, and consistent reflection, our family found its rhythm, celebrating the minor triumphs, the deep dives into subjects of passion, and most of all, the unbridled joy of discovery.

Reflection Questions:

1. How do you define meaningful learning in your personal journey and in your role as an educator or parent?

....

....

2. Think back to a time when you or someone you
know pursued learning for its own sake, not bound
by traditional markers of achievement. What insights
were gained from that experience?

....

....

....

....

3. In what ways can you cultivate a more holistic
understanding of success and learning for yourself
and those around you?

....

....

....

....

CHAPTER EIGHT

HOLISTIC LEARNING: FOSTERING MIND, BODY, AND SOUL

66

*"Education is not preparation for life;
education is life itself."*
- John Dewey

The bustling campus of my college was a far cry from the monotonous hallways of my high school. As a freshman, eager to learn and fit in, I was introduced to a myriad of ideas and concepts, many of which were foreign to my midwest upbringing. It was during a psychology class when I first stumbled upon the term "holistic." The professor emphasized its importance in understanding human development, explaining that it encompassed more than just the spiritual, contrary to popular belief.

To be honest, my initial perception of "holistic" was marred by stereotypes. Like many others, I imagined it as a "hippie" concept, limited to yoga retreats and meditation camps. Who had the time for this kind of lifestyle? But as the semester progressed, the word evolved in my understanding. It was not just about spirituality or an alternative lifestyle; it was about caring for one's entire self—mind, body, and soul. It was about recognizing that a person was more than the sum of their academic achievements or their physical appearance.

This epiphany sparked a transformation in my own life. I began to question the educational paradigms I had grown up with. The long hours spent cramming for exams, the relentless chase for higher grades, and the lack of attention to emotional well-being suddenly felt superficial. I remembered my teachers, many of whom seemed drained and unappreciated, struggling within a system that demanded results but failed to nourish their own holistic needs.

Upon graduation and stepping into the world of teaching, my enthusiasm for holistic approaches remained undiminished. Early in my teaching career, I decided to incorporate daily yoga sessions as a "brain break" for my students. I believed this would not only stretch their bodies but also clear their minds, aiding in better concentration and overall well-being. However, my attempt at integrating holistic practices into a conventional setting was met with skepticism. Some parents called, questioning why I was "wasting" precious class time. To my dismay, even the school administration seemed unsupportive, reprimanding me for stepping outside the prescribed curriculum and trying something "alternative."

Outside the classroom, I became more observant of my peers. Many were physically present, but mentally and emotionally detached, burdened by unseen pressures. The community outside the school walls, too, appeared distant, its potential to enrich our educational experience largely untapped.

The feeling of being an outlier with my holistic focus persisted, but it also shed light on a pervasive problem: the undervaluing of holistic education in our society stemmed from our traditional educational system's fragmentation of this approach. It rarely catered to the "whole" student, often sidelining emotional well-being and physical health in favor of measurable academic outcomes. My experiences both as a student and a teacher solidified my resolve: education, in its truest form, needed to nurture every facet of an individual.

hen we embarked on our homeschooling journey, the term "holistic" took on a deeper resonance than just being a contemporary buzzword. It became a heartfelt aspiration, a commitment to embrace learning in its entirety, transcending conventional boundaries.

Our transition to homeschooling was a deliberate step towards honoring education as more than a pursuit of academic achievements and percentages. Instead, we sought to transform our home into a sanctuary, a place where the boundaries of traditional education could be stretched and redefined.

We wrestled with a fundamental question at the forefront of this transition: how could we create an environment that not only nourished intellectual growth but also nurtured the emotional, physical, and spiritual facets of our children's development?

Following our decision to pursue homeschooling, it was essential to structure an educational environment that was comprehensive, touching upon every aspect of life. This was not merely about teaching subjects but fostering growth in every dimension: mind, body, and soul.

Mind

When it came to nurturing the mind in my homeschooling approach, I looked beyond traditional academic expectations. Instead of focusing solely on textbooks and memorization, my goal was to cultivate a thriving sense of curiosity. I wanted my kids to appreciate the journey of asking questions just as much as finding answers.

I created a space where thinking outside the box was encouraged. This wasn't just about absorbing facts; it was about fostering a genuine passion for discovery that would stay with them for life. In this environment, obstacles weren't setbacks but opportunities—chances for them to delve deeper, ponder, and come up with innovative solutions.

More importantly, I believed in growing a mind, not just training it. Teaching someone how to think is one thing, but inspiring them to continuously seek knowledge and understanding is another. My aim was to instill in my children an enduring love for learning, ensuring they'd remain curious and open-minded long after their formal education ended.

Embrace Dynamic Detours: Ditch that rigid lesson plan every so often. Learning can and should take scenic routes. One day, use baking to understand fractions, and another day, embark on field trips to witness history in action. With this approach, learning is always fresh and never mundane.

Schedule Brain Vacations: Recognize when your child needs a break. Just like us, children can become overwhelmed. Insert moments of pause, whether it's a brief dance-off, cloud-watching, or simply enjoying a quiet moment. These breaks can recharge and reset their minds.

Hold Curiosity Conferences: Create an environment where every question is welcomed. Be it about the colors of the rainbow or the mechanics of a toy, delve into discussions fueled by their innate curiosity. Make it a rule: no question is ever "silly."

Go on Literary Adventures: Dedicate time each day to embark on reading journeys. Dive into fantastical tales, mysteries, or inspiring real-life stories. Let the books transport you and your child to different worlds, sparking imagination and empathy.

Dive into Life 101: Transform daily chores and activities into lessons. Use a grocery trip to impart lessons about budgeting or explore botany while gardening. Every aspect of daily life can be a rich learning experience when viewed with the right lens.

Wander through Artistic Alleys: Provide ample opportunities for creative expression. Encourage your child to paint their feelings, compose a song, or craft a story. The realm of creativity not only enhances academic learning but also nurtures emotional intelligence.

Body

The well-being of the body became central in our homeschooling journey. I understood that a healthy body is the foundation for a sharp mind and a contented heart. So, we didn't just focus on typical exercises or generic physical activities; instead, we practiced and leaned into what made us feel truly alive and connected.

Nature became our primary playground. The rustling leaves, chirping birds, and the gentle caress of the wind became our daily companions. I used these moments outdoors to teach the kids the importance of staying active and in tune with their surroundings. Walking through the woods, hiking up hills, or simply observing the wonders of nature up close allowed us to appreciate our bodies and the world around us in a unique way.

More than just physical exercise, this was about understanding and caring for ourselves. Listening to when we're tired, hungry, or just need a moment of tranquility. Practices like mindful breathing, dance, or even an impromptu game of catch under the open sky became avenues for both movement and mindfulness.

My goal went beyond just the present. I wanted to instill in our children a lifelong commitment to taking care of themselves. And not just in a routine, mechanical way, but as a deeply ingrained respect and appreciation for their bodies and nature. I aimed for them to carry forward these lessons of self-care and nature-connectedness throughout their lives.

Unlock the Magic of the Outdoors: Remember, the world outside your door is a vast classroom. Embrace nature walks, backyard science experiments, or simply lie on the grass watching clouds morph. The outdoors provides unmatched lessons in science, mindfulness, and the art of observation.

Move, Groove, and Energize: Stuck on a problem? A bit of movement can shake those cobwebs loose. Whether it's a spontaneous dance session, stretching exercises, or a playful game of tag, incorporate motion to keep the energy and enthusiasm alive.

Mindful Munching: Every brain needs the right fuel. Alongside mental exercises, ensure there's a stash of nutritious snacks and hydration. Think fruit slices, veggie sticks, and water to keep the mind sharp and the body energized.

Nighttime Knowledge: The mysteries of dreams, the importance of restorative sleep, and tales of nighttime creatures could become bedtime topics. Transform sleep into an educational experience, emphasizing its importance for rejuvenation and growth.

Sit, Stand, and Learn Right: While immersing in captivating subjects, ensure the physical form isn't neglected. Regular checks on posture, alternating sitting and standing, or even ergonomic study setups can make a world of difference in long-term well-being.

Moments of Meditation and Movement: The power of mindfulness and physical well-being shouldn't be underestimated. Make room for yoga stretches, beginner tai chi moves, or simple deep breathing exercises. These activities don't just offer physical benefits; they enhance concentration, instill patience, and provide moments of tranquility amidst rigorous learning.

Soul

In embarking on our homeschooling journey, my primary goal was clear: I wanted to cultivate a peaceful home environment—one where my children felt secure and didn't feel the need to recover from. A place where their souls could flourish and guide them.

This wasn't just about helping them grow as individuals but about helping them see and understand their place in the bigger picture of life. Our focus shifted towards nurturing their empathy, compassion, and self-reflection. We sought to create a setting where they feel valued, not just for their achievements, but for who they fundamentally are.

Faith became our cornerstone during this journey. Jesus was at the heart of our homeschooling endeavors. Through prayer, we found direction, clarity, and resilience, making Christ's teachings an integral part of our daily lessons. This approach didn't compartmentalize faith as just a part of our lives; instead, it became the foundation for everything we did. This integration meant that our learning wasn't limited to academics but extended to personal faith and spiritual growth.

Morning Moments of Devotion and Worship: Begin each day with family worship and devotion. Such moments aren't just spiritual; they set an intent, infuse positivity, and help us appreciate the miracle of a new day.

Daily Gratitude Gatherings: Each day, make space for everyone to voice out one thing they're thankful for. This simple ritual can profoundly shift focus from life's challenges to its many blessings, fostering a mindset of gratitude.

Finding Spirituality in Nature: Nature, in its silent beauty, often speaks to the soul. From the soft hum of bees to the rustle of leaves, immerse in these tranquil moments. They're an avenue to reflect, appreciate, and connect deeper with life's wonders.

Open-Heart Conversations: Foster conversations centered on faith, spirituality, and God's wondrous creations. Dive into Biblical passages, share the stories of God, and navigate moral questions together. These discussions deepen faith, cultivate understanding, and pave the way for spiritual maturity.

Emotional Wellness Workshops: Remember, a strong soul often rests on emotional well-being. Regularly check in with each other's feelings. Discuss highs and lows, and celebrate the fact that every emotion has its value and lesson.

Community Compassion Projects: The joy of giving is unparalleled. Collaboratively, embark on small acts of kindness, be it neighborhood cleanups, volunteering, or even a simple act like baking for someone. These actions amplify the understanding that love, kindness, and compassion are potent tools for soul enrichment.

Through the creation and maintenance of a learning environment that could support the whole child, I watched as my children blossomed, not just as learners, but as individuals. Their resilience, empathy, and adaptability shone through, validating our decision to take this path. The moments of joy, discovery, and personal growth far outweighed any challenges we encountered along the way.

In leaving the traditional educational system, I didn't just aim to teach my children but to inspire them. To show them that learning is a lifelong journey, intertwined with every facet of our being. And as each day unfolded, it became clear that in this nurturing environment, they were thriving, not just academically, but holistically.

Yet, it wasn't just my children who benefited. This shift replenished the emptiness I had felt for so long, filling my once-depleted cup. The love, care, and holistic approach I poured into their education simultaneously became the balm that healed my own spirit. Through teaching them, I rediscovered and rejuvenated myself, affirming that true education transcends academia and nurtures the soul.

Reflection Questions:

1. Mind: How am I ensuring that my child's education nurtures their innate curiosity and love for learning, beyond just academic achievements?

   ....

   ....

   ....

   ....

2. Body: In what ways am I integrating physical well-being and nature into my own daily routine, promoting both health and a connection to the world around me?

   ....

   ....

....

....

3. Soul: How am I fostering an environment that supports not only emotional growth but also spiritual exploration, ensuring my child feels valued for who they truly are?

....

....

....

....

CHAPTER NINE

EMBRACING THE PACE: THE ART OF SLOW LIVING

66

"Nature does not hurry, yet everything is accomplished."
Lao Tzu

The morning alarm had barely rung its second note when the familiar, heart-wrenching cries of our four-month-old filled the air. As I pulled myself from the warmth of the bed, a weight settled in my chest. The day ahead promised its usual whirlwind, but the hardest part was handing my baby boy, still so new to the world, into another's arms. Entrusting a piece of my heart to someone else, while I navigated the complexities of the day, always left an ache that lingered.

Meanwhile, the rest of the house was buzzing with activity. Our two daughters, already caught in the hustle of preparing for school, needed their hair done, their bags packed, and breakfast served. Between sips of rapidly cooling coffee, I'd hear my husband, multitasking with precision, juggling his morning routine while coordinating with me to ensure none of our daughters' needs slipped through the cracks.

Every morning, my daughters and I would race together to the school where I served as principal. Despite us being in the same building, our days often felt worlds apart. They navigated lessons and playground dynamics, while my hours blurred with administrative duties and meetings. Though our paths would sometimes intersect—a spontaneous hug or a quick wave—it was clear that the roles we occupied within those school walls kept us in different spheres.

When the day's final bell heralded the end of official school hours, there was no respite. The nights mirrored our frenzied mornings with homework, dance lessons, and prepping for the inevitable repeat the next day. We all seemed to be running in different directions—and away from each other. Those rare, quiet moments with my husband dwindled to fleeting snippets, perpetually overshadowed by overwhelming fatigue. Meanwhile, genuine heart-to-heart connections with the children were condensed to hurried three-minute exchanges during bedtime rituals.

As the days blurred into weeks and months, a pattern emerged that, alarmingly, seemed to mirror the experiences of many families around us. Society appeared to have conditioned us to accept this frenzy as the norm, almost as if the chaos is a rite of passage for every modern family. "This is just how life is," people would often say with a resigned sigh, accepting the manic pace as a necessary component of contemporary living.

But a lingering thought played on my mind: what if it didn't have to be this way? What if, instead of succumbing to society's template, we could draft our own blueprint for our family's life?

It was amid this introspection and the incessant chaos of daily life that a profound realization emerged. Our lives, our routines, and even our aspirations were being dictated by the school system's schedule. Days turned into a continuous countdown to the next break, the next holiday, the next moment of respite. This wasn't the life we'd envisioned. We yearned to lean into our home's culture, to immerse ourselves in its rhythms and comforts. Most importantly, we wanted to lean into each other, to rediscover and fortify the bonds that connected us.

n our modern, bustling world, I often felt caught in the frenetic rhythm of always doing, always achieving, always racing towards some undefined finish line. The expectation was clear: push harder, climb higher, and constantly validate your worth. But in this unyielding hustle, the moments of simply being, of cherishing the mundane and ordinary, often slipped through my fingers. It was this yearning that introduced me to the transformative power of slow living, especially illuminated in our choice to homeschool.

Throughout my years in the traditional educational system, both as a student and then as an educator, there was a distinct blueprint: success was measured by external achievements. The golden report card, the accolades, and the nods of societal approval. Amid this race, life's quieter, richer moments—the unrushed breakfasts, the spontaneous laughter, the leisurely afternoon walks—often were overshadowed.

When the decision to homeschool our children emerged, it felt like a step into uncharted waters. Away from rigid timetables and the echoing buzz of school bells, we found a rhythm uniquely ours. This wasn't just a shift in our teaching approach; it was a conscious recalibration of our entire lifestyle.

As our days began unfolding at this mindful pace, I noticed subtle yet profound shifts. Our children weren't just absorbing information; they were savoring experiences. They engaged deeply with subjects that ignited their passions, unconstrained by ticking clocks.

The joy in their eyes was evident—they were learning to value the journey itself.

Our Guiding Principles to Slow Living

1. We engage in activities without succumbing to the pressure to juggle them all.

2. We embrace intentional rest, shedding any guilt associated with the absence of constant accomplishments.

3. We maintain a calendar, not as a testament to our busyness, but as a tool; we resist the urge to fill it just for the sake of it appearing full.

4. We prioritize quality time together over fleeting engagements, cherishing moments of true connection.

5. We've mastered the art of saying no, understanding that boundaries are vital for our well-being.

6. We cultivate moments of reflection, valuing introspection as much as action.

7. We immerse ourselves fully in one task at a time, practicing mindfulness and deep focus.

8. We find joy in life's simple pleasures, from a slow morning coffee to an unhurried walk in nature.

9. We nurture hobbies not for achievements or accolades but for the sheer joy they bring.

10. We engage in conversations that matter, fostering genuine connections over superficial exchanges.

11. We intentionally unplug, allowing ourselves to disconnect from the digital world and reconnect with our surroundings.

12. We practice gratitude daily, taking time to acknowledge and appreciate life's blessings, big and small.

13. We respect the natural rhythms of our bodies and minds, acknowledging that rest is as significant as work.

14. We prioritize experiences over possessions, seeking richness in memories rather than materialism.

15. We routinely evaluate our priorities, ensuring that our choices align with our values and true desires.

But the lessons weren't limited to the children. I was evolving too. In guiding them, I started reflecting upon the life practices I wanted them to cultivate. And in doing so, I confronted some uncomfortable truths about my own life. The nurturing, balanced existence I desired for them was often amiss in my own daily routine. It was a revelation.

The societal narrative, which once seemed so authoritative, began to waver in its dominance. I started understanding that incessant busyness wasn't a testament to my worth. The constant pressure to validate my existence through relentless productivity was not only draining but also unfulfilling.

When I first decided to homeschool, an inner voice whispered a paradoxical truth: "To truly succeed, I'd need to slow down." Our cultural instinct is often to fill every moment, to optimize, to multitask. But my heart told me that for my children to flourish, our homeschooling journey would need to take a different path, one less traveled. Initially, I couldn't put a name to this approach, but as time unfurled, I came to understand it as part of the "slow living" movement.

It wasn't just about pacing our lessons, but the quality of our interactions and the depth of our learning. This understanding ushered in the art of single-tasking. Rather than flit from subject to subject, we began to immerse ourselves fully in one topic, one activity, one moment at a time.

There was a day when, instead of squeezing multiple subjects into our schedule, we plunged into just one piece of poetry. We read it, dissected its meanings, acted out its scenes, and tried crafting our own verses. That day, a single poem wasn't just a lesson; it became an experience, a memory.

This wasn't just a shift in our teaching methodology, but a lifestyle transformation. Our days transitioned from checklists and schedules to explorations and discoveries. And in this new rhythm, not only did my children's understanding deepen, but so did our bonds. We weren't just covering subjects; we were living them, experiencing them together.

Single-tasking extended beyond our lessons. I found myself being more present in our conversations, truly listening to my children's words and the feelings behind them. The magic of slow living was unfolding in front of us. It was in the joy of lingering over a topic until we were satiated, the laughter over a shared joke without the rush to the next task, the satisfaction of giving a task our undivided attention.

In essence, slow living taught us that it's not about how much you do, but how deeply you engage. Through its principles, our homeschooling journey transformed from an educational quest to a life-enriching experience. The lessons of single-tasking and being present not only educated us but also shaped our very essence.

Our venture into homeschooling became more than just an educational decision; it became a pathway to rediscovery. By teaching my children the value of a balanced, holistic life, I was relearning those lessons alongside them. Each day, as we collectively chose depth over superficiality and presence over pretense, we were building a life of authentic meaning.

This journey away from the traditional school system, and into the heart of homeschooling, has been enlightening. It's taught me that sometimes, to truly move forward, we need to slow down, to reflect, and to embrace the art of purposeful living.

Reflective Questions:

1. In what ways have societal pressures influenced your own personal definitions of success and fulfillment?

   ....

   ....

   ....

   ....

2. How might embracing a slower, more intentional pace benefit not just your children's learning journey, but your own well-being and growth?

   ....

   ....

   ....

   ....

3. What steps can you take today to prioritize presence and authenticity over external validations and relentless productivity?

   ....

   ....

   ....

   ....

PART III

REFLECTIONS AND REVELATIONS

CHAPTER TEN

UNLEARNING TO LEARN: CHALLENGING PRECONCEIVED NOTIONS

66

"The ache for home lives in all of us, the safe place where we can go as we are and not be questioned."

- Maya Angelou

mbarking on a homeschooling journey after years in the epicenter of traditional education brought with it an unexpected challenge: confronting and navigating a maze of preconceived notions. Notions I had inadvertently been a part of propelling during my tenure as a principal.

The whispers of homeschooling stereotypes were not unfamiliar to me. After all, I had been on the other side of the fence for years. "Homeschoolers lack structure," "They're probably not being challenged academically," or the ever-present, "What about socialization?" Such beliefs seemed almost entrenched in the collective psyche of traditional educators. The irony wasn't lost on me when I found these very assumptions momentarily clouding my own judgment in our early homeschooling days, and speaking up against all of the misconceptions I had once played into.

An excited hush of voices and the shuffle of tiny shoes racing towards the playground filled my office. On most days, this was music to my ears—a sweet reminder of my role in shaping these young minds. But some days, this sound harbored pain from my own childhood.

I decided to step outside that day, something I'd often do to keep my pulse on the school's social heartbeat. The playground was awash with energy, a myriad of sights and sounds. But amidst the laughter and excitement, there were pockets of silence that drew me in.

At a distance, I spotted Amelia, a bright-eyed second-grader, clutching her book and looking longingly at a group of girls who were laughing and playing a game. It wasn't her solitude that struck me; it was the stark familiarity of it. A scene from my childhood days replayed in my mind, where I too, once stood on the fringes of playground politics, often left out, the sting of being "different" fresh in memory.

I approached Amelia and gently asked if she wanted to join the others. With a slight quiver in her voice, she replied, "I tried, but they said I couldn't play with them today." My heart ached as memories of my own childhood bullying resurfaced. The faces changed, the times changed, but these patterns seemed all too familiar.

I walked further and noticed, with the absence of adult supervision, small disputes turned aggressive, words thrown around carelessly, and groups formed that excluded others. The classroom rules of "no talking" and the setup of isolated desks had created an environment outside those four walls where children weren't equipped with the social tools to include, communicate, and understand one another holistically.

I explored another pocket of the playground, where I saw a student sitting on the wall as a consequence for talking with a friend during class. We often told our students to make friends, but bound them with restrictions that rarely gave them genuine opportunities to do so.

Driving home that evening, my mind replayed the scenes from recess. Coupled with the realization of the extensive homework my daughters faced that evening—and their underlying worry about the fleeting daylight hours they'd have left to enjoy—it weighed on me. Was I unknowingly playing a role in a system that fostered negative social patterns?

This thought stayed with me, serving as a poignant reminder that recognizing these patterns was only the first step. The true challenge lay ahead: making a change for my children.

~❖~

In my journey through the world of education, I've come to an enlightening realization: homeschooled children, including my own, frequently weave a richer pattern of world connections and experiences than many of their traditionally schooled counterparts. This revelation initially puzzled me. How could children, educated primarily within the confines of their homes, boast of a broader worldly exposure compared to those navigating the dynamic corridors of schools? The clues to this paradox are found in the inherent strengths of homeschooling: the luxury of time, unmatched flexibility, and—contrary to common misconceptions—a plethora of socialization avenues.

With homeschooling, I stumbled first upon that most precious and unexpected gift: time. The typical school day, often bound by rigid schedules, stood in sharp contrast to our newfound flexibility. Research suggests that a child's attention span, on average, is their age plus one minute. With this in mind, I can't help to question the logic: if, for instance, a six-year-old can genuinely focus for just about seven minutes at a time, why were traditional school days structured to be so lengthy?

In the primary years, homeschooling proved to be incredibly efficient for us. Often, less than two hours a day allowed for structured learning. This focused approach, tailored to my children's natural attention spans, allowed them to absorb information without feeling overwhelmed, while additionally allowing them the precious time to participate in social activities.

Considering the limitations of large class sizes and the impersonal teacher-to-student ratios in traditional schooling, our homeschooling environment was a refreshing contrast. We weren't pressured to move at a speed that didn't allow our family to deeply connect, dissect concepts, and build stronger relationships throughout our day.

Our learning journey extended far beyond the confines of structured lessons. Free from rigid timetables, our days took on a fluidity where learning sprouted organically. An unplanned mid-week visit to the museum, taking advantage of the peaceful weekday ambiance, or a spontaneous nature walk that seamlessly transitioned into a hands-on biology lesson—every moment held the promise of discovery. In our world, the entire day transformed into a vibrant, constantly evolving classroom.

Far from the isolation many fear, my homeschooled children have additionally found themselves intricately connected to a diverse social landscape. Their interactions span age groups and interests: from mingling with peers in community activities to engaging with seasoned mentors in specialized fields. (Can we dispel the idea that healthy socialization is sitting at a desk, surrounded by more than twenty-five peers you are told *not* to talk to during class?) These eclectic interactions, free from the typical age or grade categorizations, have not only polished their social skills but have also broadened their worldview.

While our exploration into homeschooling clarified many misconceptions around socialization, several other prevalent myths were also addressed. It was amazing to me in our first year, just how little as a society we seem to know about homeschooling, and how the ideas and concerns formed seemed to only inhibit others' interest in the idea.

Coming from a background in education, my other large concern had always been academic rigor. While former colleagues would tell me how my children were going to be "left behind," not only did homeschooling match traditional schooling in terms of academic depth, but its inherent flexibility also offered a more tailored approach to the whole child. This allowed my children to immerse themselves deeply in areas they were passionate about, pushing them beyond the boundaries that a standard, one-size-fits-all curriculum might have set.

Every moment offered a new lesson and we began to see the beauty of our world unfold. Everyday chores taught responsibility and time management, and our community outings nurtured social skills and cultural awareness. In the diverse world of homeschooling, every experience had the potential to be both educational and life-enriching.

Furthermore, the adaptable nature of homeschooling enabled us to shift gears according to my children's unique learning styles. While traditional classrooms might have students passively absorbing information, our homeschooling environment encouraged active participation, inquiry, and exploration. If one topic resonated, we dived deep, sometimes spending days or weeks on a subject until every question was satiated.

But perhaps the most significant advantage was the cultivation of critical thinking. Without the looming pressures of standardized tests and rigid curriculums, our lessons were free to roam territories that promoted questioning, reasoning, and real-world application. The narrative that homeschoolers might be at a disadvantage academically is not just outdated, but unfounded. If anything, this journey underscored the idea that learning is not just about memorization, but application and synthesis.

Remember that little girl with the overstuffed backpack and books held tightly in her small hands? The one who came home, day after day, with a spirit that seemed slightly dimmer than the morning? The vibrant child who once radiated a boundless enthusiasm for learning, only to be boxed in by a system that couldn't keep up with her pace? Today, I want to tell you about the transformation I've seen in that little girl since then.

Our homeschooling journey began out of necessity, but it quickly evolved into a choice—a choice to nurture Clara's inherent zest for knowledge, to allow her to sprint when she wanted to and pause when she needed to. The dining room table became our classroom, our garden, the laboratory, and the world around us, our playground. The shackles of a set pace, predetermined by someone who didn't know her as I did, were finally off.

Weeks turned into months, and something incredible happened. The spark that I'd seen flickering, specifically in Clara's eyes, began to shine brighter. Her questions became more profound, her explorations more daring, and her discoveries more enlightening. Our days weren't dictated by bells or strict schedules but by her curiosity.

One afternoon, as we settled into our reading nook, she shared an observation. "Mom, remember when I told you school felt slow? Now, every day feels like an adventure. I really, really love homeschooling!" Her voice, filled with excitement, was music to my ears.

But it wasn't just the academics. Clara was growing into herself. The confidence that comes from being heard, from being allowed to set one's pace, was evident in her every move. She'd hold discussions, set up experiments, and dive deep into topics that fascinated her—whether it was the mysteries of the universe or the intricate workings of a tiny insect.

One afternoon, Clara invited me into her bedroom, where she'd masterfully transformed the space into a cozy campsite. Pillows served as rough terrain, a blanket fort as the tent, and a small circle of books imitated a campfire. As I sat inside her makeshift tent, Clara recounted tales from a book she had read, her eyes dancing with vivid recollections. This was the same child who'd once said,"It's fine though,

Mom. It's like this every day." Now, every day was an exploration, a challenge, an opportunity to grow. The universe wasn't out there; it was within her, vast and waiting to be explored.

Looking at Clara now, I see more than just my daughter. I see a reflection of what education can and should be—a journey of discovery, tailored to the individual, nurturing not just the mind, but the body and soul. Today, Clara isn't just learning; she's thriving, and her spirit, once subdued by a system that couldn't cater to her, now soars freely, reaching for the stars.

Unraveling the many misconceptions of homeschooling was akin to unlearning years of conditioned thinking. Each day became a revelation, a step towards understanding that education can be, and often is, beautifully diverse. The preconceived notions that once clouded my perspective began to dissipate, replaced by a renewed appreciation for the myriad ways learning can truly unfold.

Reflection Questions:

1. Can you recall a time when you held a strong belief about a particular approach to education, only to later realize it was based on preconceived notions? How did that realization come about?

   ....
   ....
   ....
   ....

2. What stereotypes or misconceptions about alternative educational paths might you still harbor? How might you challenge these beliefs?

   ....
   ....
   ....
   ....

3. Reflect on a conversation or experience that shifted your perspective on homeschooling or any other non-traditional educational choice. What was the most impactful part of that interaction?

   ....
   ....
   ....
   ....

CHAPTER ELEVEN

THE ART OF CHANGE: WHAT MY FIRST YEAR TAUGHT ME

66

"I am always doing that which I cannot do, in order that I may learn how to do it."

- Pablo Picasso

he transition from the world of institutionalized education to the flexible realm of homeschooling was not just a change in environment; it was a transformative journey for both my psyche and pedagogy. Aside from debunking the many misconceptions of homeschooling, at every corner, there was a lesson waiting, often teaching me more than any formal training ever had.

One of the early challenges was letting go of the traditional school structure I had grown so accustomed to. The first standout was the structured timetables of school itself. The clock, which had been a relentless taskmaster dictating the flow of lessons and breaks in the school, was now just a piece of decor in our home. The idea of letting my children lead, determining the pace and direction of their learning, was both exhilarating and daunting.

I eagerly opened my new homeschool planner, freshly printed and filled with blank spaces ready to be filled with our family's learning adventures. The array of colored pens lay neatly arranged on the table, and stickers of every variety beckoned. I felt prepared, organized, and so ready to crush this new role as a homeschool mom.

With a precision that would make any educator proud, I began to block out times. Math from 9:00 a.m. to 10:00 a.m., reading from 10:15 a.m. to 11:00 a.m., and so on. Each child's day was tailored to their needs, with subjects they struggled in given more time, and breaks strategically placed. Looking at the finished schedule, a sense of achievement washed over me. This seemed foolproof.

Boy, was I wrong.

The first hiccup came early. By the second lesson on day one, one of my kids couldn't find their math book. A mere fifteen minutes later, my youngest wasn't feeling the enthusiasm for reading I had anticipated. By mid-morning, the tight schedule I created was slowly unraveling. The real-life interruptions, from a doorbell ring to a scraped knee, didn't care about my hour-by-hour plan.

By hour two of our first day, I felt like I had already failed.

It became abundantly clear: while my intentions were in the right place, I had inadvertently set an impossible standard for our days. Life, with its unpredictability and chaos, doesn't fit neatly into color-coded time slots.

The lesson I learned was invaluable: a strict schedule was not our friend. Early on, I realized the trap many fall into: trying to replicate the traditional school model at home. This, in many ways, can be the enemy of homeschool.

The beauty of homeschooling lies not in mimicking the school environment but in embracing its very antithesis. It's about creating a tailored learning experience that suits the individual needs and rhythms of our children. A flexible routine, one that allowed for life's little (and big) interruptions but still provided a structure, was the key. It was important to understand that homeschooling isn't just about academics; it's about integrating learning into the daily ebb and flow of life.

It was a humbling start, but it set the stage for a more organic, understanding, and adaptable approach to our homeschool journey. As time went on, I discovered that this flexible routine allowed for spontaneity and exploration. We could pivot our plans to chase after a sudden interest or take a break to explore a topic further. It was a liberating realization that learning wasn't confined to the walls of our home or the hours between nine and three.

Moreover, this adaptability extended to encompass our outdoor adventures. Field trips weren't limited to pre-scheduled outings but could happen on a whim. A butterfly that landed in our backyard became an impromptu lesson in entomology. A hike in the nearby woods turned into a hands-on botany class. These unscripted moments were some of the most memorable and impactful.

The fluidity of our homeschooling routine also allowed for deeper connections between my children. They began to collaborate and teach each other, learning not just from textbooks but from the exchange of ideas and experiences within our own family. These shared moments of discovery enriched our bonds and created a sense of unity that transcended traditional schooling.

As we embraced this more adaptable approach, I found myself reevaluating my own perspective on education. I realized that learning isn't a rigid march through a set curriculum but a dynamic journey filled with surprises and opportunities. Homeschooling afforded us the freedom to explore, adapt, and truly savor the joy of learning.

In addition to our shift in routines, my transformative journey included letting go of the traditional school framework that often cast failure in a negative light. Here, in our safe space, my children redefined errors not as deterrents, but as doors to deeper understanding. Each mistake was a lesson in itself, a chance to revisit, refine, and truly grasp a concept. It was heartwarming to witness their approach and, in turn, it reshaped my own perspectives on teaching and learning. True learning, as it turned out, wasn't always linear. Sometimes, the detours brought about the most profound insights.

My children's resilience was another standout. Of course, not every day was a roaring success. We had moments covered with frustration, where concepts dangled tantalizingly out of reach. There were also times when self-doubt cast long shadows, making me question our chosen path. Yet, each challenging episode became an invitation to pause, reflect, and recalibrate. These were invaluable, real-life lessons in patience and perseverance. Through it all, it became evident that the essence of learning danced to its own rhythm, one we had to respect and resonate with.

Beyond textbooks and structured lessons, my children celebrated a culture of questioning. They fostered an educational environment where curiosity was the star. They reminded me daily that the joy of learning lay not in racing to a finish line but in savoring the journey itself. Through their eyes, I rediscovered the marvels of viewing the world with wonder and inquisitiveness.

In hindsight, the biggest revelation of our first homeschooling year wasn't found in any book or lesson plan. It was the understanding that there isn't a universal "homeschool mold." There's only a "home"—and the freedom to make it distinctly our own. The journey wasn't about fitting into a pre-existing framework; it was about crafting a unique narrative that suited us, echoing the rhythms of our family and our aspirations.

~ ~

While I've continually praised the nurturing community of social media in guiding my homeschooling journey, I'd be remiss not to share a subtle challenge that intermittently crept in amidst the spectrum of awe-inspiring posts: the sly shadow of doubt caused by that ugly comparison trap.

Pictures of full and beautiful home libraries, stories of precisely planned and executed days, and elaborate lessons had a two-fold effect: on one hand, they offered a plethora of ideas, but on the other, they sometimes made me question my own methods.

One evening, as I sipped my chamomile tea, I found myself deep into Instagram. A post caught my attention—a fellow homeschooling mom had showcased her day. From a morning routine that seemed to run with graceful precision, to their afternoon filled with intentionally crafted hands-on activities and projects, it was impressive. Their day had a rhythm, a flow that looked seamless and harmonious. The children were happy, the mother rested.

It stirred a momentary unease in me. Our day had been so different. It started leisurely, had its share of messy explorations, and our routine? Well, let's just say we managed to hit all of our planned meals on time that day. Compared to the orchestrated perfection I saw online, ours felt chaotic. Was I doing enough? Should our days be more structured? Was I putting in the right amount of effort (and money) to create beautiful and intentional lesson plans?

As I reflected more deeply, I remembered our laughs, the spontaneous dance breaks, the joy of an unexpected discovery, the value of an unplanned conversation. Our form of homeschooling was a blend of structured lessons and ample space for free exploration. It was fluid, flexible, and it was uniquely ours.

It's essential to remember that homeschooling is not about replicating the traditional school model. Just as important, it's also not about copying another family's approach. Each family, each child, has their own rhythm, needs, and pace. While some thrive in meticulously planned environments, others flourish in more spontaneous settings. We can't replicate traditional school...and we also can't replicate another family's approach. The beauty of homeschooling is that there's no universally right mold—just what's right for your family.

My Biggest Takeaways from Year One:

1. **Let Life Meet Learning:** Our impromptu nature walks, baking sessions, and spontaneous discussions showcased that genuine learning was intertwined with daily life, not separate from it.

2. **Push Progress Over Perfection:** Watching my children grapple, adjust, and eventually understand a complex topic taught me that it's about the process and trial, not always getting it right the first time.

3. **Lean into Connection Over Curriculum:** Sitting down for heart-to-hearts, addressing fears, and celebrating small wins made it clear that our bond was the foundation upon which all other learning was built.

4. **Make Time for Real-Life Integration:** From balancing a budget during shopping to understanding history through family stories, it was evident that the most memorable lessons were tied to our everyday experiences.

5. **Embrace the Unscripted:** Those unplanned detours, be it chasing a butterfly or dismantling a clock, reinforced that some of the most profound lessons aren't planned.

6. **Choose Customization Over Completionism:** When one child struggled with reading but thrived in storytelling, it was a reminder that our journey was about catering to individual strengths, not just ticking boxes.

7. **Find a Balance of Planning Against Learning:** On days where meticulous lesson plans were overshadowed by a child's keen observation or question, it was clear that too much planning could stifle genuine curiosity.

8. **Choose the Journey Over the Destination:** Celebrating the small milestones, enjoying the time we had together, and stopping the endless search for a finish line, the simple, everyday moments became a journey of joy.

9. **Share in the Growth:** As my children learned new topics, I found myself learning alongside them, reminding me that education is a two-way street.

10. **Be Open to Rediscover Yourself:** Revisiting the tales of historical figures or diving into classic literature rekindled my own passion for subjects I once adored.

11. **Every Day a New Discovery:** Whether it was the joy in discovering a new bird in our backyard or understanding the physics behind a rainbow, every day held its own magical lesson.

12. **Craft Your Own Narrative:** In homeschooling, we had the beautiful responsibility of molding an educational journey that was uniquely ours.

Reflection Questions:

1. Reflect on a time when you faced a steep learning curve. How did you navigate it, and what lessons did you glean from the experience?

....

....

....

....

2. How do you respond to failures or setbacks in your personal or professional life?

....

....

....

....

3. How has your understanding of education and learning evolved over the years?

....

....

....

....

CHAPTER TWELVE

THE TAPESTRY OF MY LEGACY: THE ULTIMATE GOAL OF OUR EDUCATIONAL IMPACT

"To be yourself in a world that is constantly trying to make you something else is the greatest accomplishment."

- Ralph Waldo Emerson

y journey through education, both institutional and homeschooling, has never been just about the dissemination of information. It was, and remains, a quest to leave behind a legacy, a mosaic built from intentional pieces of passion, dedication, and love.

However, the contours of this legacy had undeniably shifted through my decision to homeschool. In the past, it was about creating lasting impacts on a larger scale, affecting policies, directing curriculums, and influencing the paths of countless students passing through the school's doors. My role as principal had granted me a unique vantage point, allowing me to envision and execute grand designs for a larger community.

Yet, at home, the canvas was smaller but no less significant. The strokes were more intricate, the colors more vibrant. The legacy here wasn't about numbers or scale; it was about depth, intimacy, and profound connection. And my pupils? My most precious gifts in life.

Thinking back once more to that bright-eyed twenty-two-year-old, stepping into a classroom, every corner of it echoed with possibility. I was hopeful, energized, and determined.

Every lesson plan I drafted, every strategy I implemented was imbued with a dream, a vision. I wanted to be more than just a teacher who imparted knowledge. I aspired to be an educator who could catalyze a complete overhaul of a system that, in many ways, had become obsolete. Naivety? Perhaps. But it was also passion, a passion that burned brighter than any challenge that lay ahead.

In faculty meetings, amidst discussions about standard procedures and curriculums, I would often find myself silently questioning the status quo. "Why not this way? What if we tried that?" The traditional mold of education seemed stifling, and I felt a relentless urge to break free, to introduce reforms that would make learning more meaningful, more aligned with the evolving world outside those classroom walls.

As years passed, the desire to influence larger systemic change led me down the path of administration. Becoming a principal was more than just a role—it was an opportunity. An opportunity to bring about the changes I had always dreamt of, to influence policies, curricula, and teaching methods on a larger scale. But with this new role came new insights, and the realization that the labyrinth of educational bureaucracy was far more intricate than I had imagined.

Despite the passion and the ideas, every proposed reform was met with layers of resistance—be it budget constraints, traditionalist mindsets, or the sheer magnitude of trying to move an entire system. There were moments of triumph, of course— instances where small changes were implemented, days when the vision seemed within reach. But those were often overshadowed by the numerous, seemingly-insurmountable hurdles.

Over time, a disheartening clarity emerged. My dream of reshaping the educational landscape, while noble, was perhaps too grand for a system entrenched in its ways. The legacy I had envisioned, of revolutionizing education from within, seemed increasingly elusive.

But the narrative that homeschooling was a "step back" or a "lesser choice" in the realms of education is pervasive. There's a profound strength in the choice to put one's family, particularly one's children, at the center of their universe. What society often overlooks is the incredible power and nobility in prioritizing the home and nurturing the next generation. Why is the choice to directly invest in one's own children sometimes seen as less valiant or ambitious? Why do we sometimes diminish the crucial role of mothers who choose to make their children their primary focus?

As I embraced homeschooling, I wasn't sidestepping my responsibility as an educator; rather, I was channeling all the passion, dedication, and expertise I had into the most personal and profound project of all—my children. Their growth, their learning, their well-being became my magnum opus. And isn't that what true education is about? Not just the broad strokes of policy changes and curricular adjustments but the deep, intimate impact on individual lives.

In dedicating myself to my children's education, I was not abandoning my broader educational aspirations but reshaping them. Through my children, through our homeschooling journey, I was laying down the foundation of an educational philosophy that, I believe, will resonate with many others. It's a legacy of love, dedication, and the unwavering belief in the boundless potential of every child.

~❖~

Every moment spent with my children has reiterated a profound truth: my legacy intertwines with theirs. Each shared laugh, obstacle, and victory echoes the depths of our homeschooling journey—a path not merely of education, but of heart and soul. It's become clear to me that if I truly want a hand in shaping my children's education and future, it's up to me to take the lead.

Looking around, it's evident: the school system, as it stands, is unlikely to transform to the degree needed during my kids' school years. We can advocate and hope for future changes, but what about the here and now? That's the reality I needed to face and act upon.

Homeschooling was never about keeping my children in a bubble or hiding them away. It was about giving them a tailored education, one that recognizes and nurtures their individual strengths and curiosities. Beyond just the books and grades, I realized that the world around them is full of endless distractions, and it's easy for kids to lose their way. By bringing their learning home, I aimed to provide a stable foundation, guiding them to stay true to their values and beliefs.

The bond between a parent and child is something unique and powerful. Through homeschooling, I hoped to harness this bond, imparting the wisdom, values, and love that an institution might overlook.

To some, stepping away from traditional education may seem like stepping back. But to me, it's a step forward. It's about committing to not only educate their minds but also to enrich their hearts and souls. It's about guiding them to become individuals with character, compassion, and clarity.

When I pause to consider the essence of education, it prompts a profound reflection: What legacy do we desire to leave for our children? For me, it's not solely about information absorption or milestones achieved; it's about empowering them to navigate the world with wisdom, compassion, and authenticity. And who could ever advocate more fiercely for a child's growth and well-being than a parent, fueled by an unparalleled love and relentless determination?

In the cozy ambiance of the café, with the rich aroma of freshly brewed coffee enveloping the air, I settled into a plush chair, cradling my own cup. Across the table, my children were engrossed in their books, occasionally taking a sip of their warm cocoa. The soft hum of conversations around us created a serene background, a kind of gentle symphony of city life.

Amid this tranquil setting, Sarah, a familiar face from our parents' group, approached our table. As she neared, I noticed a look of contemplation in her eyes. "You know," she began, her voice revealing a mix of curiosity and apprehension, "I've been considering homeschooling." She hesitated for a moment, then added, "But I'm just not sure. I mean, you have an educational background, and I...well, I'm just a parent."

It's a sentiment I hear often. Because of my prior experiences in the education sector, many assume that my transition to homeschooling was a seamless one. But that couldn't be further from the truth. Yes, I was familiar with teaching methods, curriculums, and classroom dynamics. But translating that into a home setting, interweaving the personal with the pedagogical? It presented a unique set of challenges.

Noticing the concern in Sarah's eyes—a reflection of self-doubt I had seen in my own reflection not so long ago—I posed a question to her: "Sarah, you say you're 'just a parent,' but who was the very first teacher your son ever had?"

She paused, seemingly caught off guard, and began to talk about preschools and credentials.

Interrupting her gently, I smiled, "But before all of that, wasn't it you? The parent? Weren't you the one who taught him his first words, celebrated his first steps, and patiently answered those endless 'why' questions, like 'Why is the sky blue?'"

It's a peculiar thing how our society has framed "real" education—suggesting that the invaluable teachings parents provide at home are somehow lesser than formal school teachings. Can any textbook or structured lesson plan truly capture the essence of a child as intimately as a parent who knows their every laugh, every curiosity, and every concern?

Our conversation stirred memories of my own initial apprehensions. Perhaps my uncertainty wasn't so much about my capabilities but more about society's narrow definition of both an "educator" and a "mother." Through my homeschooling journey, I've come to understand that being an educator transcends classroom walls and degrees; it's about connecting heart-to-heart, truly understanding the child, and nurturing their spirit with unconditional love.

When my children recall these years, I hope they remember more than just the lessons. I want them to reminisce about the love, the dedication, and the special moments we shared. For that, in essence, is our true legacy. It's not just about the knowledge imparted, but the bonds forged, the time invested, and the unwavering commitment a mother builds upon her children's growth.

Our homeschooling vision transcends academic metrics. It's an amalgamation of personal evolution and a commitment to fostering a brighter, more informed society. Here, education isn't about individual milestones but our collective responsibility to the world.

At the heart of this perspective is an undeniable truth: the most transformative education is nurtured in the sacred bond between parent and child. It's a convergence of knowledge, passion, expertise, and empathy, crafting a legacy that will endure.

My unwavering conviction is this: to shape a child's holistic growth and future, the parent's guidance is not only invaluable but essential.

Reflection Questions:

1. How do you envision your legacy? What do you hope to leave behind?

....

....

....

....

2. Think of someone who has left a profound impact on your life. What aspects of their legacy resonate with you the most?

....

....

....

....

3. How do our daily actions and choices contribute to the legacy we're building?

....

....

....

....

PART IV

REDISCOVERING EDUCATION'S TRUE ESSENCE

CHAPTER THIRTEEN

A FUTURE UNDEFINED: LEANING INTO THE UNKNOWN

66

"The best way to predict the future is to create it."

- Abraham Lincoln

In the sanctuary of my childhood room, a dream blossomed.

Amidst the turmoil and discomfort of school days, I found refuge in my imagination. The corner of my room, adorned with a variety of stuffed animals, became my makeshift classroom. Each teddy bear, rabbit, and lion had a name, a personality, and a backstory. For them, I was more than just their owner; I was their teacher, their protector, their friend.

With a little chalkboard propped up, I would gather my plush students around and dive deep into imaginative lessons. These sessions weren't merely child's play. To the younger version of me, they symbolized hope, a world where every student felt valued, understood, and cherished. In this world, there were no taunts or teasing, only encouragement and understanding.

As I scribbled on the board and read out lessons from my storybooks, my voice steady and filled with purpose, the outside world faded away. I'd correct Teddy for not "paying attention" or praise Bunny for her "excellent question." My lessons would be punctuated with stories from my own school experiences, but with a twist—stories where every child was celebrated for their uniqueness, where differences were embraced with love.

These teaching sessions were therapeutic. They were my way of processing the hurt, of rewriting my narrative, of creating a world where no one felt left out. Deep down, I felt an overwhelming urge to turn this fantasy into a reality. Every evening, with my stuffed animals as my audience, I fortified my resolve to change the educational landscape for children like me.

It wasn't just about escape; it was about envisioning a future. With every pretend test I graded, every story I narrated, and every question I answered, a silent promise took root in my heart. A promise that when the time came, I would be the beacon of hope for others, that I would provide a haven similar to the one I had crafted in my room.

School, for me, may have been a battleground, but my heart and soul were set on a mission. The dream that took flight amidst my stuffed animals would shape my destiny. The resilience I learned as a child would fuel my passion as an adult. For in my heart, I knew: my purpose was to create a world where every child felt seen, heard, and above all, loved.

rom the earliest days of my career, planning was embedded in my DNA. As a principal, the realm I navigated was one of constant foresight. Predicting challenges, crafting solutions, and laying down strategies was all in a day's work. This wasn't just a professional trait—it was an intrinsic part of who I was. I thrived on creating roadmaps, not just for my school, but for my life. Every milestone, be it personal or professional, was carefully charted out, every twist and turn anticipated. The joy I found in planning stemmed from the clarity it brought, the semblance of control over an unpredictable world.

When I embarked on the homeschooling journey, I was introduced to a wholly different perspective. Here, my meticulously drawn plans often met the whimsical and wondrous detours of child-led exploration. Homeschooling wasn't just about ticking boxes or following a linear trajectory. It was about allowing space for serendipitous discoveries and embracing the beautiful chaos of organic learning. This journey taught me that while plans offer direction, it's the unplanned moments that often hold the most profound lessons.

As I adapted to this new rhythm, a question consistently lingered in the backdrop: *what about the future?*

Early on, that whisper was thick with anxiety. I'd find myself lying awake, bathed in the soft glow of the nightlight, ruminating. I'd think about my kids—what if they ever wanted or needed to return to a traditional school setting? Had we equipped them well enough to make that transition? And beyond that, were the values, knowledge, and skills they were absorbing at home truly on par with what life would later expect of them?

Then there was the reflection on my own journey. Having been a principal, my career was intrinsically tied to the education system. Choosing a path divergent from it wasn't just a personal decision; it felt like a professional statement. I believed in what we were doing, and every fiber of my being told me this was right for our family now. But I couldn't shake off the looming questions about the implications of our choice for the days ahead.

Every family has its unique rhythm, and for now, homeschooling was our perfect tune. But when my gaze shifted from our present cocoon to the vast horizon of the future, there was a mix of hope and hesitation. Was this beautiful journey we had embarked on laying a robust foundation for whatever paths my children, our family, and even my own career might take in the years to come?

Despite the constant uncertainty and the endless questions, a few things slowly began to clarify in my mind. I watched my kids. I saw their curiosity blossom, their resilience strengthen, and a fiery passion for knowledge light up their eyes. It hit me then: the future isn't just some distant point we're racing towards; it's built daily, through every experience, every mistake, every lesson learned.

And you know what gave me solace? Seeing the intangible values my kids were internalizing. Realizing that, perhaps, success isn't solely defined by traditional academic benchmarks or societal standards. It's about the heart, the character, the journey.

I didn't toss out planning for the future—oh no. But my approach morphed. It became less about setting fixed markers for success and more about nurturing foundational principles. I wanted my kids to have an insatiable hunger for knowledge, to possess the agility to pivot when life threw curveballs, to have a grounded sense of ethics, and the tenacity to face and conquer challenges.

With these core values as our guiding lights, the looming shadow of the future began to feel less threatening. It started looking like a vast expanse waiting for us to make our mark. Whether my kids later opt to dive back into traditional education, chase after college degrees, explore the realm of startups, or even venture into paths less trodden, I have this unwavering belief: they're equipped, not just with knowledge, but with the spirit and determination to carve their niche and thrive.

"Mommy, what do you think I will be when I grow up?"

The question, ever-so-innocent and sparkling with curiosity, has echoed in my ears countless times. Each repetition fills me with a poignant mixture of emotions. It's a joy stemming from the trust my children place in me, seeking guidance and envisioning their vast futures, and a reflection on the immense possibilities that lie ahead for them, waiting to unfold.

When my husband and I made the pivotal decision to homeschool our children, we found ourselves immersed in a similar introspection. Behind closed doors, we'd often wonder aloud, discussing and dreaming about what the future might hold for each child as they matured. What would homeschooling mean for them as adults? How would this path shape their aspirations, their personalities, and their trajectories in life?

Beyond academics, beyond the milestones society often places undue emphasis on, what were the true treasures I wished for them to carry forward from their homeschooling experience?

At the heart of it, I yearned for them to possess a trauma-free childhood. A childhood free from the pressures of conforming, from the shadow of unnecessary competition, and from the weight of external judgments. In essence, I wanted to provide them a sanctuary, an environment where their self-worth wasn't dictated by report cards or peer validations, but by the strength of their character, the kindness in their hearts, and the depth of their passions.

This didn't mean I wanted to shield them from challenges. Quite the contrary. I hoped for them to face difficulties, to stumble occasionally, but always within a safety net of understanding, guidance, and love. By experiencing setbacks in an environment anchored in support, they would learn resilience, not from theoretical lessons, but from lived experiences.

One of the most profound aspirations I held was for them to emerge from their childhood with a deeply rooted sense of self. Homeschooling, in its essence, was our shared journey to ensure that they weren't molded into societal templates but had the space and support needed to grow into the unique individuals they were destined to be. I hoped that the lessons, experiences, and memories we created would serve as a compass, helping them navigate the vast oceans of life with confidence, grace, and authenticity.

I often envisioned them as adults, looking back at their homeschooling days. My deepest wish was for them to recall these years with fondness, to remember the laughter, the tears, the discoveries, and most importantly, the freedom. The freedom to be themselves, to explore without judgment, to make mistakes and learn from them, and to foster dreams that weren't limited by conventional boundaries.

In creating their futures, my overarching mission was not just to prepare them for the world but to inspire them to be individuals who could inspire and change the world themselves. To be trailblazers who recognized their innate potential and harnessed it for greater good.

Stepping into the role of a homeschooling mother, I was often enveloped by a haze of questions and self-questioning. The responsibility of guiding a classroom of students is one challenge, but shaping the entire educational path for your own child is a deeply personal and intense commitment. Every decision felt magnified, every step heavy with consequence, sometimes blurring the joy of this chosen path.

But through this intricate labyrinth, I unearthed an inner strength, anchored by the deep-seated love and aspiration I held for my child's future. While I couldn't sketch out every detail of their upcoming journey, I was armed with an irreplaceable asset: a steadfast belief in their capabilities and an undying will to be their strongest ally. This very epiphany fortified my confidence as a homeschooling mom.

My journey towards self-assuredness was marked not by leaps, but by subtle, treasured moments: the gentle curve of my child's smile signaling comprehension, the zest with which they'd dive into new learnings, and the triumphant gleam in their eyes after overcoming a hurdle. Each day, these moments solidified my faith in our shared journey, nurturing the trust I held in my instincts and capabilities.

To every homeschooling parent navigating this terrain of introspection, here's my message: your dedication to your child, the depth of love that drives you in this educational voyage, is your true north. Even if the road seems foggy and the future uncertain, take heart in knowing that your undying commitment is your child's greatest advantage. In this beautiful, complex journey, you stand as your child's most unwavering champion.

As we continue this journey, I am reminded that our role as parents is not to predict the future for our children. It's to equip them with the tools, values, and passion to create their own future. A future undefined by societal norms, but illuminated by personal aspirations, dreams, and purpose.

Reflection Questions:

1. How do you view the future? Is it a set path, or an evolving journey?

....

....

....

....

2. What guiding principles do you believe are essential for navigating an uncertain future?

....

....

....

....

3. Reflect on a time when you had to adapt to unforeseen changes. What did you learn about yourself and your ability to shape your own destiny?

....

....

....

....

CHAPTER FOURTEEN

FROM COMPLIANCE TO PASSION: REKINDLING THE JOY OF LEARNING

66

"Education is not the filling of a pail, but the lighting of a fire."
- W.B. Yeats

emember those early days of toddlerhood? When every pebble was a treasure, every bird's song a concert, and every cardboard box a castle. Little eyes filled with wonder and little hands eager to touch, feel, and discover. Every moment was a learning experience, driven purely by curiosity, not compulsion. It was a time when learning was innate, instinctual, and above all, joyful.

But somewhere along the way, this changes for many. By the time kids hit the "compulsory education" age, a subtle yet significant shift occurs. As society starts its clamor about "kindergarten readiness," a cloud shadows the brilliance of natural curiosity. No longer is learning driven by wonder; it becomes about compliance.

When we first ventured into homeschooling, having come from a structured school environment, our family faced an unexpected challenge: deschool. It wasn't just the kids; it was me too. For years, we had been conditioned into a routine that was driven by bells, schedules, and external expectations. Our perception of success was skewed, revolving around grades, approval from authority figures, and societal benchmarks.

Our Steps to Deschool:

Deschooling is often mistaken as a mere pause, a brief interlude between traditional schooling and homeschooling. But in reality, it's a transformative period—a metamorphosis of both the learner and the educator.

1. **Pause and Reflect:** Before jumping into homeschooling, take a moment. Understand why you're transitioning. Talk with your child about their school experiences, both good and bad.

2. **Embrace Free Play:** Allow ample time for unstructured play. Let your child rediscover hobbies, interests, or even simple outdoor play without time constraints.

3. **Open Dialogue:** Make it a routine to have open conversations about feelings, experiences, and expectations. Understand your child's perspective on learning and school.

4. **Limit Academic Pressures:** Step back from structured academics. This might mean no formal lessons for a while. Allow natural questions and curiosities to guide learning.

5. **Rediscover Learning Together:** Go on educational outings of mutual interest—perhaps a science museum, an art exhibit, or nature walks. Learn side by side.

6. **Introduce Variety:** Expose your child to various learning resources beyond textbooks—documentaries, puzzles, DIY kits, and interactive websites.

7. **Establish a Safe Space:** Make sure your home environment is conducive to open expression, where there's no fear of judgment or penalties for wrong answers.

8. **Connect with Others:** Engage with homeschooling communities or support groups. It helps to share experiences and gather insights from those who've been on the same journey.

9. **Ditch the School-at-Home Mindset:** Understand that homeschooling isn't about recreating the classroom at home. It's about crafting a unique, tailored learning experience.

10. **Trust the Process:** Understand that deschooling doesn't have a set timeframe. It might take weeks or months, and that's okay. Trust in your child's pace and your own journey as an evolving educator.

Note: The reflection questions found at the end of each chapter in this book were built to further aid your mental deschooling process.

For my eldest daughter, math had always been about ensuring she was meeting grade level, looking for solutions by any means possible for the sake of tests, and not for the pleasure of growth or problem-solving. My other daughter's creativity in writing was often stifled, adhering to specific formats instead of letting her imagination run wild. And me? I was always on the clock, trying to fit learning into neatly compartmentalized slots of time.

The first months of our homeschooling journey were as much about unlearning these conditioned responses as they were about discovering new ways of learning. We had to shed the skin of "traditional" expectations and norms. We started by reclaiming reading, diving into books without the pressure of comprehension questions or quizzes, and simply enjoying the narrative. We worked real life math problems; we penned stories without the confinement of strict structures.

Bit by bit, as we peeled away the layers of traditional schooling, we began to see the reemergence of that innate joy of learning. We began to rebuild our foundation, not on compliance and rigid standards, but on passion, curiosity, and connection. And in doing so, we didn't just find a new way to educate; we rediscovered the joy and wonder that had drawn us to learning in the first place.

From my early days in the field of education, I prided myself on being a perpetual student. I believed in modeling the love for learning, advocating the idea that one should never stop absorbing, understanding, and growing. Yet, as the years went by, amidst the hustle of the educator's life, my love for learning underwent a silent transformation.

Professional development sessions, workshops, and courses started dictating my learning trajectory. Instead of choosing subjects that ignited my passion, I found myself enrolling in sessions because they were mandated, or because they'd add a feather to my professional cap. I was caught in a cycle of learning for the sake of credentials, rather than for the pure joy of it. Somewhere along the line, compliance overshadowed curiosity.

The realization of this shift didn't dawn upon me immediately. It was a gradual understanding, akin to slowly waking up from a deep slumber. It took the transformative journey of homeschooling, a path of rediscovering the essence of learning, for me to confront my own detour.

As I watched my children immerse themselves in subjects they loved, driven by pure enthusiasm and wonder, I was struck by a poignant contrast. Their learning was unadulterated, uninfluenced by external validations. It was here, in the middle of our homeschooling sessions, that I remembered the sheer joy that learning once brought me. It was a wake-up call, reminding me of the difference between learning out of genuine interest and learning out of obligation.

It was time for a change. I decided to reclaim my title of "evergreen learner," but with its original essence. I started with crochet. It may seem like a simple, perhaps even trivial choice, but for me, it was profound. There was no end goal, no certification awaiting, just the pure joy of creating with my hands, making mistakes, unraveling, and starting again. The intricate patterns, the feel of the yarn, the satisfaction of seeing a project come to life—it was therapeutic. It was learning in its most organic form.

Emboldened by this experience, I ventured further. I continued to search for topics that piqued my interest—not because they were required for my profession, but because they fascinated me. Ancient civilizations, the art of storytelling, the science behind essential oils—my learning palette expanded, and it was colorful, diverse, and immensely satisfying.

Homeschooling, in its essence, was not just an educational choice for our children, but a door that led me back to the love of learning. It reminded me that education, stripped of its societal expectations and pressures, is a beautiful journey. It's about chasing curiosities, embracing challenges, and reveling in the process. And as I rekindled my love for learning, I found myself setting an even more powerful example for my kids. It wasn't just about words and advice; it was about living the philosophy of being a true evergreen learner.

In our schools today, there has been an all-too-familiar shift from the pure, uninhibited joy of learning to a more structured, compliance-driven approach. For many students, learning has become synonymous with meeting benchmarks, scoring grades, and adhering to prescribed curricula. But buried beneath this avalanche of expectations and regulations lies a fundamental truth: at its heart, learning is a journey of discovery, a passion-fueled exploration of the vast landscapes of knowledge.

Over the years, the systemic emphasis on compliance has, unintentionally, dimmed the intrinsic enthusiasm learners naturally possess. When classrooms transform into assembly lines of information dissemination, and students become mere vessels awaiting content, the true essence of education is overshadowed. The metric-driven methodologies, while effective in producing quantifiable outcomes, often sideline the emotional and intellectual engagement that makes learning truly transformative.

Rekindling the joy of learning means fostering environments where questions are celebrated, where exploration is encouraged, and where mistakes are viewed as stepping stones rather than setbacks. It's about creating spaces where learners aren't just passive recipients but active participants in their educational journey.

In this transformative approach, the home emerges as a powerful epicenter of such a holistic education, and the parent as guiding educator, plays an indispensable role. The familial bonds, the intimate knowledge of the child's strengths and passions, and the inherent desire to see them thrive provide a foundation that traditional dynamics simply cannot replicate.

Moving education back to the home, the boundaries between formal and informal learning are not only blurred, but also harmoniously intertwined. In this setting, every moment becomes an opportunity for discovery and growth.

I've always felt most at home in the quieter moments of life. As an introvert, crowded places and unexpected encounters tend to catch me off guard, pushing me momentarily out of my comfort zone. So, it was with mixed feelings that I stumbled upon a familiar face from my previous school while out on a routine errand.

The Thompsons were always one of those families that exuded warmth. Even amidst the most challenging days as a principal, their genuine smiles and understanding nature were like a soothing balm.

In a sea of faces that sometimes blurred together, theirs always stood out—radiating kindness and positivity.

But seeing them outside the confines of school, especially after my difficult departure, sent a rush of conflicting emotions. There was the joy of seeing friendly faces, but also the trepidation of potentially opening old wounds. As our eyes met, any hesitations quickly melted away. Mrs. Thompson approached with her characteristic grace, her children trailing behind with eager waves.

The conversation started with the usual pleasantries, dancing around the giant elephant in the room: my sudden exit from the school. But as we spoke, Mrs. Thompson's gaze frequently shifted towards my children, who were immersed in a book they had just picked up. It was evident; she noticed the spark in their eyes, the eagerness with which they discussed their recent projects with her children. Their joy in learning, rekindled through our homeschooling adventures, was palpable, impossible to miss.

"Your children seem so...happy, so engaged," she remarked. And as I shared our adventures, our switch to a child-led learning approach and the lessons we've learned, a beautiful thing happened. The space between us—once filled with unsaid words and unaddressed emotions—became a bridge of understanding and inspiration. Her questions about homeschooling weren't just out of politeness; they were rooted in a deep desire to understand, to maybe even consider it for her own family.

Our conversation ended with heartfelt goodbyes and promises to stay in touch. But it was what transpired a few months later that truly touched my heart.

A message notification pinged on my phone. It was Mrs. Thompson. Her words flowed with the same warmth and grace that I remembered. She shared how our chance encounter had left a lasting impression on her. How she had spent nights researching, contemplating, and discussing with her husband. And finally, they had made the decision: they were going to embark on a homeschooling journey.

Reading her message, tears welled up in my eyes. Not just because they had chosen this path, but because that chance meeting had showcased the transformative power of homeschooling. Our encounter had not only rekindled a connection but also bore witness to the potential and beauty of a personalized education. The Thompsons' decision was more than just a choice for their family; it was a testament to the profound impact of homeschooling.

Reflection Questions:

1. Reflect on a moment when you learned something significant outside a traditional educational setting. What made that lesson memorable?

....

....

....

....

2. How can we foster an environment, whether at home or in schools, that encourages experiential learning?

....

....

....

....

3. In what ways can everyday experiences be transformed into educational opportunities?

....

....

....

....

CHAPTER FIFTEEN

A JOURNEY HOME: REDISCOVERING MYSELF THROUGH THEIR EYES

66

"The greatest discovery of all time is that a person can change by merely changing their attitude."

- Oprah Winfrey

Growing up, my world was limitless, an expansive realm of dreams, discoveries, and delightful curiosities. With every sunrise, a new adventure beckoned, promising a day of exploration, wonder, and sometimes mischief. I was the embodiment of youthful exuberance—always questioning, always imagining, always seeking.

The trees in our backyard weren't just trees. They stood as towering guardians of secret realms, with branches that whispered tales from long-forgotten eras. My favorite spot under a particular oak became a sanctuary, where I'd read, imagine, and even hold "councils" with my stuffed animal companions. Every stone, every ripple in the creek nearby, every rustling leaf was part of an intricate tapestry of tales, and I was the eager listener, absorbing their stories with wide-eyed fascination.

The summers felt endless, with days spent riding bikes and playing catch, and evenings spent catching fireflies. Rainy days had their own charm, with the pitter-patter of raindrops drumming a rhythmic backdrop to the stories I'd write or masterpieces I would paint.

But as the sands of time flowed, the free-spirited, inquisitive child began to fade into the background. The enchanting world of limitless possibilities started to be replaced by the practicalities and structures of adulthood. As I transitioned into the educational system, first as a student with high ambitions and later in my professional role, the vibrancy of those childhood days began to dim.

The weight of responsibilities, the demand for conformity, and the pursuit of a structured career path painted over the vivid tapestries of my youth. Instead of the world being a vast canvas of wonder, it started to feel more like a set of boxes to be ticked, goals to be achieved, and standards to be met.

I began to miss that little girl, the one who found magic in the mundane, who could spend hours talking to the wind and listening to the whispers of the universe. The one who believed that anything was possible if you dared to dream it.

Yet, life has its way of coming full circle. As I embarked on the journey of homeschooling my children, fragments of that past began to shimmer through the present. Through my own children's wonder-filled eyes, the magic I thought I had lost was rekindled. The stories, the adventures, the limitless dreams— they all returned, reminding me of the profound simplicity and joy of childhood.

It was a poignant reminder that while we might grow up and the world around us might change, the essence of who we once were remains, nestled deep within, waiting for the right moment to sparkle again. But even more, it was a beacon for the path I hoped to pave for my children.

efore embarking on this homeschooling journey, my identity had been, in many ways, interwoven with my professional role. "School Principal," "educator"— these weren't just titles; they were a facet of who I was.

But another transformation was quietly taking place—the rediscovery of myself through my children's eyes.

It started subtly. Observing them, I began to see reflections of my younger self—the fiery spirit, the insatiable curiosity, and the boundless energy. Through their questions and observations, I was reintroduced to aspects of myself I had inadvertently shelved away in the hustle of administrative responsibilities and societal expectations.

One day, as we were delving into a literature lesson, my daughter remarked, "You always seem to get lost in stories, just like I do." That innocent observation was a gateway to memories of my childhood, where books were my sanctuary and stories my escape.

Another instance was during a science experiment. My quirky ten-year-old, observing my excitement, commented, "You're just like a big kid, aren't you?" It was said in jest, but it held a profound truth. The childlike wonder, the thrill of discovery, the joy in the little things—they were all there, waiting to be relit.

These moments weren't just about nostalgia. They were reminders of the core essence of who I was—an essence that, while evolving, remained constant. It was a realization that, beneath the roles, titles, and responsibilities, the core self remains.

When people discover my past as a school principal, there's an almost predictable rhythm to the subsequent conversation. First, a hint of surprise

in their eyes, followed by a myriad of questions about managing a school and the challenges that come with it. But there's one question that invariably surfaces: "Don't you miss being a principal?"

It's a fair question. The role, undoubtedly prestigious, commanded respect, influence, and a sense of authority. The corridors echoed with a certain reverence, children greeted with a mix of admiration and apprehension, and every decision I made rippled through the very fabric of the school community. It was a position that many aspired to and, quite honestly, one I took great pride in.

When I made the shift, my parents processed through a cocktail of emotions—pride, bewilderment, and concern. "Are you sure about this?" they'd gently ask.

Friends were taken aback, and colleagues simply couldn't fathom it. "You had such a promising career ahead," they'd muse, shaking their heads in disbelief. "Why walk away from it all?"

But the truth is, while the title brought with it a sense of achievement, it also carried an invisible weight. The long hours, endless meetings, paperwork, and the ceaseless balancing act of managing teachers, students, and parents—it was a whirlwind that left little time for anything else. And while I was immensely passionate about my role, I often felt trapped in a labyrinth of administrative duties, far removed from the core essence of education and my passion of purpose.

What people don't realize is that my decision to leave was less about walking away from a title and more about walking towards something more profound—a journey of authentic connection, both with my own children and the essence of learning.

Now, when I wake up each day, it's not the ringing of the school bell or the impending meetings that guide my day; it's the pure, unadulterated joy of learning and growing with my children. Each day presents a canvas, where lessons aren't dictated by a syllabus but inspired by curiosity.

So, when asked if I miss being a principal, my response is simple: I miss certain moments, certain people, and certain challenges. But do I regret my decision? Not for a single heartbeat. For in this new chapter, I've rediscovered the magic of learning, unburdened by titles or expectations. I've found a space where my heart feels light, my spirit feels free, and every day holds the promise of a new adventure.

So no, I don't miss being a principal. I cherish the memories, value the experiences, but I've found a path that feels infinitely more fulfilling—a path where education isn't just a profession but a way of life.

As I rediscovered these facets of myself, I also began to understand my children better. Their dreams, fears, hopes, and aspirations mirrored mine, albeit in different contexts. This mutual rediscovery deepened our bond, making our educational journey together even more enriching. As we explored subjects, we also explored ourselves, learning, growing, and evolving together.

Things I've Learned From My Children:

1. **Endless Wonder:** Through their eyes, I've relearned the joy of marveling at the simple things, realizing that the world is still filled with wonders waiting to be discovered.

2. **Strength in Vulnerability:** Their openness in sharing their fears and joys has shown me that being vulnerable is not a weakness but a profound strength.

3. **The Power of Persistence:** Watching them tackle new challenges has reminded me of my own inner resilience and the value of pushing forward, even when the path gets tough.

4. **Authenticity Is Gold:** Their genuine reactions and emotions, unfiltered by societal norms, have emphasized the importance of staying true to oneself.

5. **Value of the Present:** Their innate ability to be in the moment has taught me the richness of experiencing the now, without constantly looking ahead or behind.

6. **Imagination Unleashed:** Observing their boundless creativity has reignited my own imaginative spirit, showing me that age doesn't dim the flames of imagination.

7. **Embracing Mistakes:** Through their trial and error, I've learned the grace of accepting mistakes and the growth that comes from them.

8. **Deep-Rooted Empathy:** Their innate compassion for others, be it a friend or a stray animal, has reinforced my belief in the innate goodness of the heart.

9. **Unwavering Curiosity:** Their constant questions have not only expanded their knowledge but have also made me question and understand the world in new ways.

10. **Joy in Simplicity:** They've shown me that the most profound joys often come from the simplest moments, be it a shared laugh or a story told under the stars.

11. **The Courage to Dream Big:** Their dreams, unhindered by the practicalities of the world, have inspired me to reach for my own, no matter how lofty they might seem.

12. **Deep Connections Matter:** More than anything, they've emphasized the value of genuine connections, teaching me that relationships, when nurtured, can be life's biggest treasures.

13. **A Fresh Perspective:** With every shared discovery or new insight, they've given me a fresh lens to view the world, constantly challenging my preconceived notions.

Let's be honest, our fears as parents often stem from deep-seated misconceptions. We fear our children might fall behind, that they won't fit the conventional mold, or that we might fail them as educators. These misconceptions, more often than not, are born from our own insecurities, and it's essential to confront and dispel them. I realized that it's not just about teaching my children but also unlearning my own preconceived notions and fears. I didn't gain my confidence in our homeschooling journey until I fully embraced it, until I jumped in. And in doing so, I hope to instill in my children the assurance that they can be confident in every step they take, always.

The clarity and insight I gained from this journey into homeschooling were transformative. It made me realize that I didn't want my children to wait until adulthood to discover themselves or find their purpose. No, I wanted them to seize the present, to live a life that's wild, free, and uninhibited by societal norms, right now.

As parents, and as lifelong learners, we hold the pens that write our children's stories. But rather than writing for them, let's provide them the space and trust to craft their own tales, their own discoveries. In their narratives, let's ensure chapters filled with wonder, adventure, and the freedom to explore, question, and grow.

Our children's education is more than just about academics; it's about shaping souls ready to engage with the world with empathy, enthusiasm, and authenticity. This, after all, is the heart of homeschooling. It's not just about teaching; it's about inspiring, it's about understanding, and most importantly, it's about love. And in this journey, I found that while I set out to educate my children, it was they who ended up teaching me the most invaluable lesson: the power and beauty of learning and living without bounds.

Reflection Questions:

1. Have there been moments in your life when you've seen yourself through someone else's eyes? How did that make you feel?

   ....

   ....

   ....

   ....

2. How can reconnecting with our core essence benefit our relationships with our children or learners?

   ....

   ....

   ....

   ....

3. Where will you let education take you?

   ....

   ....

   ....

   ....

EPILOGUE: FULL CIRCLE

"In the end, we'll all become stories."

- Margaret Atwood

From the hallways echoing with the all-too-familiar ringing bells and student chatter to the serene, sometimes chaotic, corners of our home dedicated to learning, my journey has been nothing short of transformative. But as I stand at this juncture, reflecting on the pages of our story, I realize that every chapter, every twist, has been leading to a profound realization: the heart of education is not in structures, systems, or syllabi—it's in the souls we touch, the lives we impact, and the futures we shape.

Leaving my role as a principal wasn't just a professional shift; it was a personal awakening. And as our homeschooling journey unfolded, with its myriad challenges and triumphs, the line between educator and mother blurred. Instead, a new identity emerged: a guide, a mentor, a lifelong learner alongside my children.

This journey brought into sharp focus the inherent flaws of a system that often prioritized uniformity over uniqueness, benchmarks over individual brilliance. It wasn't just about my microsystem or the larger educational system; it was about the very essence of what education means in our society.

But amidst these reflections and revelations, there was also hope. If a former principal and her children could break the mold, redefine educational norms, and craft a journey so deeply personal and transformative, then perhaps there's hope for change on a larger scale. Perhaps our story could be the beacon for others to chart their own courses, to challenge the status quo, and to rediscover the true essence of learning.

Homeschooling was never the end goal; it was the vehicle. The destination was, and remains, a deeper connection—to my children, to myself, and to the very essence of education. The destination was understanding that true learning is not confined within walls or bound by curriculums; it's a lifelong pursuit and ever-evolving journey of discovery.

As I pen these final lines, I am filled with immense gratitude. Gratitude for every challenge that shaped us, every question that guided us, and every moment that defined us. And as this chapter concludes, another begins—a chapter filled with promise, potential, and endless possibilities.

For in the end, our story is not just about education; it's about love, resilience, discovery, and the indomitable human spirit. It's a testament to the power of belief, the strength of conviction, and the boundless possibilities that lie ahead when we dare to chart our own course.

Thank you for journeying with us.

APPENDIX A:
REFLECTIONS & EXERCISES

Introduction:

The following exercises and reflections are designed to help readers delve deeper into their own educational experiences, beliefs, and aspirations. They can be used by individuals, in group discussions, or as a foundation for journaling.

1. Mapping Your Educational Journey

Reflect: Consider your personal journey through education, both as a student and perhaps as an educator or parent. What were the pivotal moments that shaped your beliefs and feelings about education?

....

....

....

....

....

....

Exercise: Draw a timeline of your educational experiences. Mark the highs and lows. Next to each, jot down a brief note about why that moment was significant.

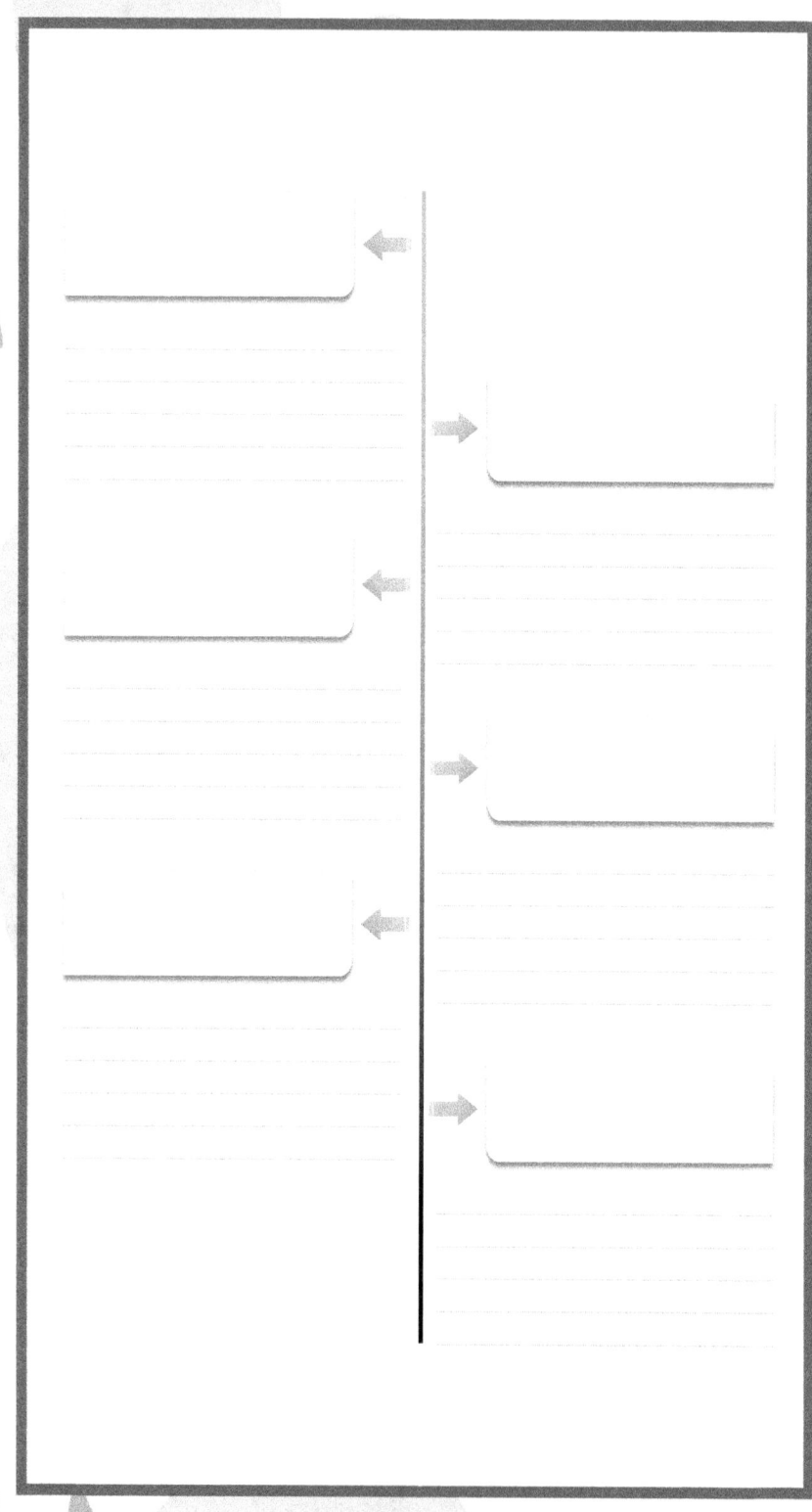

2. Defining True Education

Reflect: What does true education mean to you? Beyond Academia, what values, skills or experiences do you believe are essential for a well rounded education?

What does **true** education mean to you?

Values

Skills

Experiences

Exercise: Write a personal definition of education in 100 words or less.

ed·u·ca·tion
/ˌejəˈkāSH(ə)n/

noun

   1.

3. The Role of Schools

Reflect: Consider your experiences with the traditional school system. What are it's strengths and weaknesses in shaping you or your children?

<u>Strengths</u>

<u>Weaknesses</u>

Exercise: List five positive and five negative aspects of traditional schooling. For each negative, brainstorm a possible solution or alternative approach.

Positive Aspects of Traditional Schooling

....

....

....

....

....

....

....

Negative Aspects of Traditional Schooling

....

....

....

....

....

....

....

....

4. Homeschooling Insights

Reflect: If you were to homeschool (or if you already do), what would be your primary motivation? What reservations might you have?

Reservations

Reservations

Primary Motivation

Reservations

Reservations

Reservations

Exercise: Create a SWOT (Strengths, Weaknesses, Opportunities, Threats) analysis as a new (or veteran) homeschool parent.

STRENGTHS	WEAKNESSES

OPPORTUNITIES	THREATS

Strengths

....

....

....

....

....

....

....

Weaknesses

....
....
....
....
....
....

Opportunities

....
....
....
....
....
....

Threats

....
....
....
....
....
....

5. Rediscovering Passion in Learning

Reflect: Think about the times in your life when you felt most passionate about learning. What sparked that passion?

....

....

....

....

....

....

....

....

....

....

....

....

....

....

....

....

....

....

Exercise: Identify three topics or skills you'd love to learn or explore further. Create a basic plan for how you might dive into each

1.

I want it because...

My first steps forwards diving in are:

2.

I want it because...

My first steps forwards diving in are:

3.

I want it because...

My first steps forwards diving in are:

6. The Power of Community

Reflect: How has community (or the lack thereof) impacted your learning experiences or those of your children?

My Community Goals:

Exercise: Identify three ways you can foster a sense of community in your (or your child's) educational journey, whether in a homeschooling context or otherwise.

7. Challenging the Status Quo

Reflect: In what ways have you felt compelled to challenge the established norms in education? What barriers have held you back?

....

....

....

....

....

....

....

....

....

....

....

....

....

....

....

....

....

....

Exercise: Write a letter to your younger self, offering advice, encouragement, and insights about education based on what you know now.

8. Vision for the Future

Reflect: Where do you see the future of education heading, both in a broader societal context and in your personal life or family?

....

....

....

....

....

....

....

....

....

....

....

....

....

....

....

....

....

....

Exercise: Craft a vision statement for your ideal educational environment or approach, looking five years into the future.

Our Homeschool Vision Statement

9. Mission for the Future

Reflect: Understanding your vision of education for your family, how will you achieve it? What steps will you take, and what does this timeline look like?

....

....

....

....

....

....

....

....

....

....

....

....

....

....

....

....

....

Our Homeschool Mission Statement

Closing Note:

Education is an evolving journey, and our perceptions and beliefs about it are deeply personal and influenced by myriad factors. Use these reflections and exercises as a starting point, and don't hesitate to adapt them to better fit your unique context and experiences. Remember, the path to authentic education is paved with introspection, curiosity, and a willingness to challenge the norm.

APPENDIX B:
STEPS TO TRANSITION TO HOMESCHOOLING

Embracing homeschooling is not merely a shift in venue—from school building to home—but represents a profound transformation in our perspective towards education itself. As we transition, it's essential to recognize and unlearn many of the conditioned beliefs and practices we've grown accustomed to in the traditional education system. This phase, known as "deschooling," is crucial for both parents and children. The process helps shed rigid structures and encourages a holistic, more fluid approach to learning.

In the following sections, I've laid out steps for parents and children to embark on this transformative journey focusing on the mind, body, soul, the art of slow living, and some practical considerations. Each step serves as a guidepost, helping you to realign, recalibrate, and rediscover the joy of learning in its most authentic form.

For Parents:

Deschooling Your Mind:

☐ Reflect on your own school experiences—both positive and negative.

☐ Challenge long-held beliefs about learning and schooling.

☐ Journal about what you wish your own education had included.

☐ Read literature on alternative education methods.

☐ Listen to educational podcasts or webinars.

☐ Recognize that learning isn't limited to textbooks or classrooms.

☐ Detach from the idea that learning happens within specific hours.

☐ Understand that each child learns at their own pace.

☐ Appreciate the value of unstructured learning.

☐ Let go of the need for constant measurable outputs.

Deschooling Your Body:

☐ Prioritize physical health: adopt a balanced diet and regular exercise.

☐ Ensure adequate sleep for energy and clarity.

☐ Practice deep-breathing exercises for stress relief.

☐ Engage in activities that aren't explicitly "educational"—dancing, painting, or cooking.

☐ Go on nature walks, observing without a set agenda.

☐ Adopt habits that encourage physical freedom.

☐ Embrace tactile learning—get hands dirty in the garden, clay modeling, etc.

☐ Incorporate movement in your day, e.g., stretch breaks.

☐ Prioritize self-care: take baths, meditate, or have a quiet cup of tea.

☐ Listen to your body: rest when tired, eat when hungry, and move when restless.

Deschooling Your Soul:

☐ Engage in deep introspection.

☐ Recognize and combat fears related to your child's future.

☐ Foster a strong inner connection through faith and mindfulness.

☐ Prioritize emotional and mental well-being.

☐ Create a vision board for your homeschooling journey.

☐ Seek supportive communities or groups.

☐ Establish clear boundaries to guard your family's peace.

☐ Engage in activities that bring joy and fulfillment.

☐ Allow space for growth, making mistakes, and self-forgiveness.

☐ Embrace gratitude daily.

Embracing Slow Living:

☐ Set aside specific days with no plans—let the day unfold.

☐ Engage in activities that require patience, like gardening.

☐ Declutter physical spaces to encourage mental clarity.

☐ Set intentional screen-time boundaries.

☐ Foster hobbies that aren't goal-oriented.

☐ Prioritize quality time over quantity of activities.

☐ Practice mindfulness, being present in every moment.

☐ Opt for nature trips over rushed touristy activities.

☐ Engage in slow arts like knitting, pottery, or woodcraft.

☐ Simplify routines and schedules.

Practicalities:

☐ Set realistic expectations for the deschooling process.

☐ Clear out school-like materials.

☐ Document the deschooling journey, noting changes and progress.

☐ Attend homeschooling seminars or workshops.

☐ Seek mentorship from veteran homeschooling parents.

☐ Visit alternative learning spaces or communities.

☐ Introduce your family to the idea gradually.

☐ Dedicate a space in your home for free exploration and learning.

☐ Consider financial implications and budget accordingly.

☐ Revisit and reassess goals periodically.

~❖~

For Kids:

Deschooling the Mind:

☐ Express any worries or fears about leaving traditional school.

☐ Talk about favorite and least favorite subjects.

☐ Read books of choice, without any "lesson" tied to them.

☐ Discuss personal learning preferences and styles.

☐ Explore topics previously deemed "too advanced" or "too simple."

☐ Forget grade levels and focus on interest levels.

☐ Watch educational shows or videos purely for fun.

☐ Engage in critical thinking and open-ended questions.

☐ Embrace creativity without boundaries.

☐ Understand that learning can be fun and not just task-oriented.

Deschooling the Body:

☐ Prioritize play—unstructured and imaginative.

☐ Integrate more outdoor time, regardless of weather.

☐ Take up a physical sport or activity like swimming, cycling, or hiking.

☐ Listen to the body's rhythms: nap when needed, eat when hungry.

☐ Explore various art mediums: drawing, painting, sculpture.

☐ Dance without structured steps or routines.

☐ Participate in hands-on DIY projects.

☐ Practice yoga or other calming physical activities.

☐ Experiment with different craft projects.

☐ Visit different natural terrains: beaches, forests, mountains.

Deschooling the Soul:

☐ Express emotions openly.

☐ Engage in age-appropriate meditation or mindfulness exercises.

☐ Maintain a personal journal to jot down feelings.

☐ Connect with nature on a spiritual level.

☐ Discuss personal aspirations and dreams.

☐ Foster empathy and compassion through community service.

☐ Participate in group discussions or circles.

☐ Explore different cultures, religions, and spiritual practices.

☐ Create a personal vision board

ABOUT THE AUTHOR

Mandy Davis is more than just an educator; she's a revolutionary voice in the educational arena. From the bustling hallways of a school where she served as a principal, to the vast digital corridors of Instagram where she interacts with her 100K-strong community, Mandy's mission has always been clear: transforming education in ways that empower students and families.

With her extensive background in education, Mandy has seen firsthand the challenges and triumphs of the educational system. This intimate understanding, combined with her innate drive, has propelled her into the spotlight as an advocate for a more personalized, empowering, and enriching educational experience.

Her thought leadership has not gone unnoticed. Major news outlets like Fox News and the NY Post have regularly featured her insights, echoing her passion and dedication to a wider audience. Further solidifying her status as an educational thought leader, Mandy was recognized in LA Weekly's "Top Ten Innovative Educators in the US," an accolade that speaks volumes of her relentless commitment.

Beyond media appearances, Mandy has taken her message to stages across the country. Her poignant address at the sold-out 2023 Wild + Free conference left attendees deeply moved, inspired, and ready to take action.

But at the core of all her achievements is Mandy's unwavering belief in the boundless potential of every student and the role of educators and parents in unlocking that potential. Through her words, both spoken and written, she's not just sharing a philosophy— she's igniting a movement. Join her as she continues her journey, challenging norms and reshaping the future of education.

ACKNOWLEDGMENTS

Writing is an intimate endeavor, a pouring out of the soul onto pages, but this journey of expressing my heart in words was far from solitary. Sharing these chapters, these thoughts, these moments—it's a testament to a collective effort, to the many hearts and hands that have touched and shaped my story.

To my husband, my confidant, and my sounding board—thank you. Whether it was for bouncing ideas, sifting through drafts, or simply being the calming presence when the weight of words became too much, I owe so much of this book's existence to you. Your belief in this story, in our story, has been the pillar upon which these pages stand.

To my children, you are the inspiration, the muse, and the very heartbeat of every word penned. This narrative, while mine, is also an ode to you, to us, and to our shared journey.

To Bryndle Shaver, dear friend and the artistic genius behind Homebuilt Education, thank you for your unmatched ability to weave aesthetics and creativity into everything we do. Your gift transcends the timeless simplicity of the beautiful cover and journal design; it's the aura, the feeling, the very essence of our brand. Without your creative lens, my vision would be incomplete.

To Ainsley Arment, your unwavering encouragement has been a beacon in moments of doubt. You've constantly reminded me to believe in my mission, my voice, and the change I wish to bring. The faith you've shown in my journey has been a grounding force, urging me to push forward even on the rockiest paths.

To my parents, extended family, and friends who have stood by, supported, and believed in this project from its nascent stages to now, your support means the world.

And lastly, to HMDpublishing, Clara, Mark, Matt, and the entire publishing team who worked diligently behind the scenes, ensuring that every aspect of this book resonates with perfection—thank you. Your efforts have breathed life into my words.

Works

Body, Mind and Spirit. (n.d.). Learning for Justice. https://www.learningforjustice.org/magazine/spring-2005/body-mind-and-spirit

Clingan, G. (2022, October 25). *Seeing Myself Through Your Eyes*. Collective World. https://collective.world/seeing-myself-through-your-eyes/

Comer, J. P. (1997, July 1). *The Home-School Team: An Emphasis on Parent Involvement*. Edutopia. https://www.edutopia.org/home-school-team

How do you socialize homeschooled kids? | Outschool. (n.d.). Outschool. https://outschool.com/articles/homeschool-what-about-socialization

How to Be a Confident Homeschool Mom(5 Ways to Feel More Self Assured). Practical Mommy Life. (2020, April 1). https://www.practicalmommylife.com/become-a-confident-homeschool-mom/

Kristine, L. (2021, March 30). *lean into the unknown — — Lola Kristine*. Lola Kristine. https://www.musicoflola.com/blog/2021/3/11/lean-into-the-unknown

Prensky, M. (2021, March 16). *The Goal of Education Is Becoming (Opinion)*. Education Week. https://www.edweek.org/leadership/opinion-the-goal-of-education-is-becoming/2014/05

Roe, A., Blikstad-Balas, M., & Dalland, C. P. (2021, January 26). *The Impact of COVID-19 and Homeschooling on Students' Engagement With Physical Activity*. Frontiers in Sports and Active Living; Frontiers Media. https://doi.org/10.3389/fspor.2020.589227

Smith, A. (2022, September 27). *Student-Driven Learning: Igniting Passion Through Community Connection*. Prichard Committee for Academic Excellence.

Specialist, A. K. S. S. S. O. (2023, September 7). *Blended Learning Vs. Traditional Learning: A Detailed Overview Of The Two Approaches*. eLearning Industry.

The Illusion of Education. Life in a Blog. (2013, October 14). https://aakashtyagi.wordpress.com/2013/10/14/the-illusion-of-education/

The Ultimate Guide to Structured and Unstructured Learning. London School of Emerging Technology. (2023, August 14). https://lset.uk/blog/the-ultimate-guide-to-structured-and-unstructured-learning/#:~:text=Rigid%20Path%20Towards%20 Your%20Goals,strict%20with%20a%20specific%20 progression.

Ward, K. (2019, December 17). Study shows smaller class sizes are not always better for pupils. MSUToday | Michigan State University. https://msutoday.msu. edu/news/2019/study-shows-smaller-class-sizes-not-always-better-for-pupils

What is child-led learning? (n.d.). Touch-type Read and Spell (TTRS). https://www.readandspell.com/what-is-child-led-learning

A FINAL NOTE:

Embarking on this homeschooling journey and sharing it with you has been nothing short of a profound experience. The pages of this book may have reached their end, but our collective journey as a community of passionate educators and parents is just beginning. I'd love to continue this dialogue, to learn from your stories, insights, and experiences, and to share more of what unfolds in our homeschooling adventure.

Here's how you can stay in touch and join me on this ever-evolving journey:

Email: For personal stories, questions, or sharing insights: info@homebuilteducation.com

Instagram: For daily snippets, inspirations, and a look into our homeschooling world: @homebuilteducation

Website: For weekly blogs, articles, resources, and more: www.homebuilteducation.com

YouTube: For videos, tutorials, and a visual journey into our homeschooling life: www.youtube.com/@homebuilteducation

From the bottom of my heart, thank you for taking this journey with me. Let's continue to inspire, uplift, and support one another as we redefine the boundaries of education and nurture the boundless potentials of our children.

With deepest gratitude,

Mandy

www.ingramcontent.com/pod-product-compliance
Lightning Source LLC
Chambersburg PA
CBHW070659130626
46553CB00005B/1775